The Liberated Mind

Throwing off the Bonds of the Past and Finding Freedom in Christ

Dr. Edwin J. Derensbourg III

The Liberated Mind

Dr. Edwin J. Derensbourg III

Printed in the United States of America
ISBN: 1-56229-476-8

Pneuma Life Publishing
P. O. Box 1127
Rockville, MD 20849-1126
(301) 251-4470
(800) 727-3218

Internet: http://www.pneumalife.com

Contents

Dedication

This book is dedicated to the descendants of African people who were victimized and enslaved physically and mentally by the lies, deceptions, and cruel treatment of the Europeans. Captured and brought to America, we were reduced to the less than human institution of slavery. It is time for us to throw off our mental chains and realize the destiny God has purposed for us. *"It is time."*

Acknowledgments

To my wonderful wife Venita, for such loving support and encouragement.

To my children, Joy, Jeana, Matthew, Naomi, and Edwin IV, who constantly remind me of my responsibility and obligation to future generations.

To Marie Heard for her diligence in compiling and editing the manuscript for this book.

To Derwin Stewart for the blessing he's been in encouraging me to get this work out to the Body of Christ.

Special Thanks

Special thanks to the saints of Abundant Life Christian Ministries of Hi Vista, who have been such a great support. All pastors should be blessed with the privilege of leading such a loving, supportive, devoted, and appreciative congregation.

Preface

Teaching biblical and historical truth about the contributions of the African people to the world was not an easy thing for me to start doing. In fact, I never imagined my ministry would head in this direction. During an otherwise uneventful trip, however, God opened my eyes to some startling truth and put a new vision in my heart.

While my wife and I were resting on Catalina Island, a friend shared some biblical black history with us. As we read these books, we looked at each other in amazement. I said, "Honey, how can I teach this to our congregation?" Because I pastored people from other cultural backgrounds, the need for sensitivity posed an even greater challenge to me. After two years of studying our heritage, the Lord led me to step out in faith and address this issue.

What was my biggest problem? I didn't want to offend anyone who was not black, but I knew I needed to bring forth many truths that had been concealed for years.

During those two years of study, God made some adjustments in my attitude and prepared me to be a vessel for the transmission of truth. I felt a little awkward at first because I also went through a lot of psychological warfare. Trying to get my own thoughts lined up with the truth was indeed a struggle.

I had a growing conviction that God wanted me to present the truths that are now found in this book. What's more important, however, is *how* we present truth. Because I wanted people to hear me and receive what I said, my heart and attitudes had to be free of anything that would turn people away from the message God had given me.

We can't eradicate racism if we are racist!

I also discovered how people, both black and white, fight against the truth.

Black people have practically accepted what their oppressors have projected onto them. In fact, I have fielded complaints from blacks after teaching on biblical and historical black history. The good news, however, is that my message has also been received by whites.

After teaching a series of radio messages about the injustices faced by Africans in America, I received a phone call from a white television studio in Lancaster, my home town. They had heard my broadcasts and wanted to know if I would be interested in presenting them on television.

If your message is the truth, those with a heart for truth won't have any problem receiving it. The vessel presenting the truth must be free from wrong attitudes. If the messenger has a pure heart, those in the audience will have less difficulty in receiving the truth. Even your best efforts, however, may meet with opposition.

After teaching a message on "Rediscovering Our Inheritance," I received a phone call from a white sister in the Lord. She said I offended at least three other whites that particular Sunday. I simply told her, "What I said was the truth. The problem is not with me but with the truth. That means you have a problem with Jesus Who is Truth, not me." Because I had done nothing but bring forth the truth in a spirit of love to my African brothers and sisters, I recommended that she talk to Jesus about what was troubling her.

Biblical, historical truth has a way of reaching deep and exposing things that are not right in a person. My sister has since gotten prayer and is past that incident.

As delicately as you may try to handle truth, many times the truth will stir up things in order to make one free. It may be temporarily painful, but your freedom is worth the price. Allow these pages to renew your mind and open new possibilities to you. As you become all that God intended you to be, the world will be a better place.

Foreword

Just one trip to a bookstore reveals thousands of titles. Books promise cures for loneliness, sexual problems, martial problems, mental illness, crime, alcoholism, and a myriad of other ailments afflicting humanity today. All these volumes have one thing in common. They agree that mankind is in trouble.

Beyond that one point, however, there is no accord regarding what can be done to repair lives damaged by these afflictions. I believe one cannot begin to prescribe effective cures until making an accurate diagnosis of the real nature of the problem. In this book, Dr. Edwin J. Derensbourg III has diagnosed the needs of humanity.

Unlike historians and biblicists, most people are not convinced that we can avoid repeating the past by knowing the past. Indeed, the very idea of the United States of America is based on the concept of escaping the past and making a fresh, new start. This has too often led to a mindless celebration of our history rather than a serious review of that history. This realization does not necessarily change the value of the insights to be gained from such a review.

In *The Liberated Mind*, Dr. Derensbourg has shown us the contrast between the workings of mankind's conscious and unconsciousness mind and how we can distinguish between the two. The author calls our attention to the pulling down of strongholds in the conscious mind in an effort to expose prolonged bondages and to promote freedom through knowledge of the truth.

This book blends biblical theology, solid psychology, and practical common sense. Dr. Derensbourg writes about anger, guilt, depression, inferiority complex, and pseudo-perfectionism, which is that constant and pervasive feeling that we are never "good enough." Taking us to the heart of lingering emotional pain, he shows how we can find permanent freedom from our inner turmoil through the truth of God's Word. Dr. Derensbourg believes that the faith of the Christian can transform impossible situations into possible ones; darkness and hopelessness into light and optimism.

This book avoids simplistic answers, pious condemnation, and confusing jargon. Instead, Dr. Derensbourg writes with compassion, graciousness, and understanding. Throughout the book he intersperses warm anecdotes about real people. His writing reveals a sensitive person who is at ease imparting biblical truth through his use of the Word of God and in his dignified counseling of troubled, searching people.

Because I deeply respect Dr. Derensbourg's ability to stir the minds of thinking people, I approached his book with high expectations and did not come away disappointed. I am grateful for the privilege of recommending this book and do so enthusiastically.

William LaRue Dillard, Ph.D.
Pastor/Teacher/Author
Second Baptist Church
Monrovia, California

Introduction

The purpose of *The Liberated Mind* is to delve more deeply into the problems that plague people today. Since the writing of my first book, I have seen how strongholds keep precious people struggling, not knowing or understanding what they are dealing with. Many of the problems that I have observed in people are based on lies they have received and believe to be true. Demonic strongholds may need to be broken in their lives; even after the demonic spirits have been cast out, however, the mind of the one set free must be transformed in order to remain free.

Benjamin B. Wolman writes, "The human mind is divided into what one is aware of, i.e. his conscious or consciousness and what he is unaware of, or his unconscious. The unconscious is divided into preconscious and unconscious proper. The preconscious includes all that one has in his mind but not on his mind at a particular moment."[1] This book examines deep strongholds in the unconscious mind to expose what's there and bring deliverance to longstanding bondages.

The unconscious mind works like the hard drive of a computer. The hard drive has the capacity to store information that can be retrieved when someone outside of it presses the correct keys. When someone manipulates the proper programmed function, what's stored in the hard drive will surface.

Reverend F. Earle Fox, author of *Biblical Inner Healing*, writes:

The unconscious is that upon which we rely in order to attend to something else. That means that the unconscious is, as it were, the "ground" upon which the conscious stands. In that sense the past is the ground upon which our present stands. The past is the accumulation of all these lessons we have stowed away and rely upon. Education is largely the conscious programming of the unconscious. Much of that stowed away is unconscious and long forgotten but operating down below just the same, like the engines in the bowels of an ocean liner. The captain on the bridge does not think much about the engines, but he is glad they are there.[2]

After some time, what you have learned becomes a way of life and such a part of you that you don't consciously think about what you are doing.

Another example of how the unconscious mind works can be seen in the tying of one's shoe. You can tie your shoe and hold a conversation with someone without really thinking about your shoelace. In other words, you have so mastered the task of tying your shoes that you can attend to other things without being distracted.

The musician who has mastered his instrument can focus on the melody while his fingers seem to unconsciously know what notes to play.

So, like a computer hard drive, our minds are very capable of pulling up data stored years ago in our brain. Long-forgotten experiences, however, can continue to affect us today. Scripture gives us this warning:

See to it that no one misses the grace of God and that no bitter root grows up to cause trouble and defile many (Hebrews 12:15, NIV).

Because of the conscious and unconscious programming of the mind, many today have long-forgotten traumas and abuses that spring up and cause trouble, not only in their lives but in the lives of others.

I will concentrate on hidden things and on issues that have surfaced in the minds of all people. The family's influence, along with environmental influences, play a tremendous role in the molding and shaping of our thinking and the way we approach life. I will also examine the psychodynamics of deep mental bondages as they relate to us as African Americans. Psychodynamics is "the study of the mental and emotional processes, underlying human behavior and its motivation, especially as developed *unconsciously* in response to environmental influences."[3]

Our environment has exposed us to images and symbols that have helped to shape our thinking and the way we react to life. Distorted images and symbols can and will cause us to approach life in a way that hinders our potential from being fully developed and expressed. Instead of being actors, we become reactors in response to images and symbols we have internalized. The wrong concepts and patterns of thinking that many have internalized must be removed in order to view God, self, and others in a proper way, based on truth and not distorted interpretations biased by man's opinion.

I have had the privilege of counseling many people who have experienced tremendous deliverance in their lives. Some of their testimonies have been included to encourage you that these principles do work to bring lasting change.

I believe that people in and out of church are looking for genuine help and have grown weary with superficial solutions. When you are in bondage, you can shout and dance in church for only a short time. After the shout and dance are over, there is a reality check. Like Lazarus, you may have been raised to life, but you soon discover that you're still bound hand and foot with a napkin covering your face (John 11:44). The emotional high of worship is only temporary, and people need something real and permanent.

I will look at the problems and solutions through God's Word. My goal is to bring deliverance to the captives and sight to the blind. After the lies and deceptions have been exposed and truth is set in place, then we can see the manifestation of what our Lord prayed:

My prayer is not for them alone. I pray also for those who will believe in me through their message, that all of them may be one, Father, just as you are in me and I am in you. May they also be in us so that the world may believe that you have sent me.

I have given them the glory that you gave me, that they may be one as we are one. I in them and you in me. May they be brought to complete unity to let the world know that you sent me and have loved them even as you have loved me (John 17:20-23, NIV).

From one man he made every nation of men, that they should inhabit the whole earth; and he determined the times set for them and the exact place where they should live.

God did this so that men would seek him and perhaps reach out for him and find him, though he is not far from each one of us.

'For in him we live and move and have our being.' As some of your own poets have said 'We are his off-spring.'

Therefore, since we are God's offspring, we should not think that the divine being is like gold or silver or stone – an image made by man's design and skill (Acts 17:26-29, NIV).

Reverend F. Earle Fox sums it up well:

God is more interested in where we are going than in where we have come from. Our primary focus needs to be present and future oriented, not past. Our focus needs to be purpose, rather than cause oriented. But there are causes to deal with in order to fulfill our purposes. We will not get where we are going if we are dragging a hundred pound ball and chain out of our past.[4]

Let's lay aside every weight and get ready to run the race with endurance (Hebrews 12:1).

A Dream

As I slept, I dreamed. I seemed to be climbing a hard, ascending track and just behind me labored one whose face was black. I pitied him, but hour by hour he gained upon my path. He stood beside me, clothed in power, and then I turned in wrath.

"Go back!" I cried.

"What right have *you* to stand beside me here?"

I paused, struck dumb with fear,

For Lo! the black man was not there – But Christ stood in his place!

And oh, the pain,

the pain,

the painful look from His dear face!

I will take rejection, and I will take the wounds, my son. And in the midst of it all, I will put in you a backbone of *steel*,

and a forehead of flinty *rock* –

that you may set forth the *truth*

in the midst of a rebellious and deceived generation.

. . . And a way of *rejoicing* shall reverberate from your stirring – while at the same time, weakness and impurity shall attempt to shut it down, but it shall only have a loud sound, and nothing more. It shall only be as a mouse attempting to sound the lion's roar.

See it as such ... and laugh with Me,

blessed

and chosen son of favor.

Anonymous

Chapter One

Building Upon a Lie

When people operate outside the truth, nothing is left but lies. The Bible clearly says, "the truth shall make you free" (John 8:32). Lies, however, will keep you in bondage. Jesus Christ, who declared Himself "the way, the truth, and the life" (John 14:6), made this scathing remark to the Jews who opposed Him:

> You belong to your father, the devil, and you want to carry out your father's desire. He was a murderer from the beginning, not holding to the truth, for there is no truth in him. When he lies he speaks his native language, for he is a liar and the father of lies (John 8:44, NIV).

In order to become what God has intended us to be, we must remove all lies and establish truth as the foundation in our lives. Jesus told us that acting on truth puts us on solid ground.

Whosoever cometh to me, and heareth my sayings, and doeth them, I will shew you to whom he is like: He is like a man which built an house, and digged deep, and laid the foundation on a rock: and when the flood arose, the stream beat vehemently upon that house, and could not shake it: for it was founded upon a rock (Luke 6:47,48).

A house is only as stable as its foundation. In order to establish a foundation that will support the structure of our lives, we must dig deep.

Jesus also warned what will happen to structures that lack a secure foundation.

But he that heareth, and doeth not, is like a man that without a foundation built an house upon the earth; against which the stream did beat vehemently, and immediately it fell; and the ruin of that house was great (Luke 6:49).

Without a foundation, the house couldn't withstand the rains and floods. Notice that the storm beat on both structures. What made the difference in the fate of the two houses? The foundation upon which each house rested.

In order for people to become strong and withstand the storms of life, they must dig below the surface of their lives to get to the real issues. Every lie must be completely removed so that a solid foundation of truth can be established.

That means that I can't build my house on a lie because lies have no substance. There's no substance because lies are not real. Lies have replaced truth in many people's hearts simply because the truth is not always easy to handle. In fact, the truth may make you miserable before it makes you free!

Lies cover and suppress the truth. The Word of God cautions us against those who "suppress the truth by their wickedness" and who "exchanged the truth of God for a lie" (Romans 1:18,25, NIV). Lies appeal to the flesh and our carnality.

Why Embrace a Lie?

People who do not walk with Jesus Christ easily embrace lies. Truth challenges us to change, and people hate change. Truth exposes lies that have made you comfortable. Truth convicts you of sin. (See John 16:7-14.) Because people hate change, they prefer to keep the lie. When they embrace lies, however, they turn their backs on the Spirit of Truth.

People have been lied to early in life concerning who they are and where they came from. Many lies have been told, consciously and unconsciously. It's terrible that these lies were spoken. What is more devastating, however, is the fact that many people accept these lies as truth.

People embrace lies in order to protect themselves from painful and hurtful experiences. Dr. Stan DeKoven, author of *I Want To Be Like You, Dad*, shares about being verbally abused by his father when he was a young boy. After trying to impress his father by painting the fence, he heard these words:

> 'If you're going to do a man's job, you need a man to do it. Stan, you're never going to amount to ——!'

> My only way to defend myself from this painful word was to change the meaning of it. Unconsciously, I rerouted the message, telling myself, 'He had a bad day. He didn't really mean it. I never liked painting anyway, so it really doesn't matter.' I distorted the message, replacing the truth with a lie to survive.[1]

Dr. Stan DeKoven needed to cope with his hurt, so he embraced a lie to ease the pain.

Many have buried painful situations in lies. That faulty foundation of lies begins to haunt us as we interact with others. Until we uncover the lie and remove it, we will continue to be unstable. There is no stability in a lie.

The Flat Table

Reverend Earle Fox, in his book, *Biblical Inner Healing,* gives an example of a table used for accurate measurements.

There is, I am told, at one of the major aerospace establishments in New England, a room insulated from sound and temperature changes, and from physical disturbances, containing a special table. The table is made of stone or metal, which has been machined to be as flat as human technology can make it. The margin of error is so small as to be barely detectable. Perhaps nothing on earth exists which is so flat as this table. The purpose of the table is to provide a base for making extremely small and extremely accurate measurements in the design and production of airplane engines.

The table functions like a standard measuring rod, such as one might find at the Bureau of Standards in Washington, DC or in London or Paris. The Bureau of Standards holds a measuring rod which is arbitrarily chosen as the "true foot." It becomes the standard by which all other measuring feet are judged. If someone should sneak in and shave a fraction of an inch off the standard or bend the rod, there would be great consternation. For if the standard measuring rod is no longer true, then, theoretically at least, there is nothing left by which to bring it back into true. When the basic measuring standard is twisted, it is as though truth itself has been twisted. The error would compound upon itself, for any attempt to correct the error would have to be made by measuring instruments which were themselves not perfectly true. Likewise, if the measuring table were to sustain a warp, any measurements made from it would be faulty, and the products made from such measurements would not function as they were intended. If a foundation built for a house is not even, then any walls built on that foundation are not likely to form square corners as the walls and ceiling meet.

Human life is full of conditions where value judgments have to be made. Value judgments are like measurements in technology. They have to start from a stable and true foundation. Otherwise the judgments that come forth will not be trustworthy.

There is a compulsive drive in humankind to find an objective standard for doing things. We want to know what is really right and what is really wrong.[2]

I agree with Reverend Fox. In order to get true and accurate measurements, we must start from a stable and true foundation.

People in and out of the church are trying to build, measure, and stabilize their lives by things that are not stable, true, or accurate. *They're trying to build upon a lie!*

In order for us to know right from wrong, we must have some standard to measure right from wrong. To know the truth, I must have something whereby I can measure what's true and what's false.

A Warped World

The Bible declares that "all have sinned" – not some – "and come short of the glory of God" (Romans 3:23). "The heart is deceitful above all things, and desperately wicked: who can know it?" (Jeremiah 17:9).

David wrote, "Behold; I was shapen in iniquity; and in sin did my mother conceive me" (Psalm 51:5). Our very shape or nature is formed in wrong doing. That's why you don't have to teach a baby how to sin or lie. It's his or her nature at birth. Scripture says we "were by nature the children of wrath" (Ephesians 2:3).

When we examine worldly philosophies and psychological theories, we begin to understand why the world is so warped and unstable. The "father of lies" has sent a lying spirit to permeate our world and promote deceit and destruction (John 8:44, NIV).

What are some of these lies? We can find the meaning of life within ourselves. Other lies promote self-realization and self-actualization. In other words, we don't need to look to anyone outside of ourselves to find our purpose, destiny, and an understanding of how to live with fulfillment.

The world has cut itself off from the tree of life and is on a collision course with death. People in the world are trying to help one another with inaccurate and unstable means. Jesus said it best: "If the blind leads the blind, both shall fall into the ditch" (Matthew 15:14). That's why the therapist has a therapist! When your therapy is over, did you know that your therapist may be seeking help also?

People can't find the final resting place for their emotional pain and hurt. Each person finds someone else to dump on. We simply pass around our sin and sickness to one another, never getting healed and released by the power of God.

Let me restate the problem: No one can within himself become that flat table or measuring rod by which all others can be measured with stability and accuracy. Why? Because "all have sinned, and come short of the glory of God" (Romans 3:23).

Healing Our Brokenness

The world offers a measure of help through therapy and support groups. Therapy from unbelievers has helped many to expose unconscious conflicts and rediscover their wounded inner child, but ultimately it takes the power and grace of God to cleanse and heal us of our brokenness, not repetitious confessions reminding us of our past failures. Our confessions must be founded in truth, based on the testimony that Jesus left us in His Word.

What do we need for proper care? A sure foundation! (Isaiah 28:16). We need a tried stone – a stone that's accurate and stable. Someone who won't move after I leave, seeking help for himself. Someone to whom I can go and from whom I can receive all the therapy I will ever need.

No one on earth can make you completely whole because no one on earth is completely whole. We need the truth, and the truth is a person – Jesus Christ!

Until we come to Truth Himself, we will continue to build on a lie.

Only one standard exists by which we can measure right and wrong, truth and lies – that standard must be the Anointed One and only begotten Son of God. Jesus Christ paid the price to put an end to the suffering and bondages people face today. In order for anyone to be freed from the lie, however, he or she must be open to truth.

Probing and using hypnosis to treat a client's suppressed regressions can invite dangers once they have surfaced. The secular therapist doesn't have all the tools to bring proper healing. The client risks having traumas and hurts surface with which they are not emotionally or psychologically prepared to handle. All too often the therapist recommends drugs in order to cope with events that cause deep emotional hurt and pain.

We believe that God can do a better job through the healing power of the Holy Spirit.

Over the past ten years in ministry we have prayed for many who were trying to build their lives and their relationships on a lie. One sister in the Lord with whom my wife had the privilege of praying shared her testimony with us. We would like to share it with you.

Velma: The Lie Before Birth

One Sunday afternoon, as the pastor concluded a message on "Issues of the Heart," the Holy Spirit ministered to me. During the altar call the pastor asked us to go back to our childhood memories, back to our mother's womb by the leading of the Holy Spirit. Was there anything that may have caused us to feel rejected? I went up for prayer and the Holy Spirit revealed the following:

When my mother was pregnant, she was carrying twins but did not know it. As time went on, she was told by many people that she was having twins; however, the doctors' examinations, tests, and x-rays showed only one baby and a fibroid growing alongside the baby. Simultaneous heartbeats also indicated only one baby, not two. As months went by, the fibroid grew as much as the baby. Still no signs or possibility of twins. During the last month of my mother's pregnancy, the doctors were concerned that the fibroid had grown so much that the baby was at risk. Therefore, they prepared to induce labor in order to save the baby and attempt to remove the fibroid. A specialist suggested another x-ray to determine the exact position of the baby before surgery. Ultrasound was not available in those days. The final x-ray showed there were two babies – not one. Twins were born two days later.

Since the Holy Spirit revealed this to me and not to my twin sister, I know that I was the baby referred to as a fibroid; my sister was the baby they expected all along. I was wrongly identified as a fibroid – not as a human being. Maybe this explains why I had always felt a void and an emptiness. Although I was loved very much and given lots of attention, the root to my void was rejection.

I was born with several childhood illnesses; my sister was perfectly healthy. I had a disease of the lip called hemangioma, a benign tumor made up of blood vessels that typically occur as a purplish or reddish, slightly elevated area of skin. At that time, no known medicine could cure this disease. Radiation treatments eventually cleared it after a year.

Second, I was bow-legged, completely deformed. Both legs were put in a cast and a metal bar attached to both ends of the casts. This helped my legs to heal faster, allowing them to be strong enough when I started walking.

Third, I had extremely sensitive skin. Constant rashes left marks even after my skin had cleared. Throughout my elementary years it was worse, and I developed a complex. These rashes covered my body, especially my legs. This caused me a great deal of embarrassment throughout my childhood.

It's ironic that 30 years later, I went through symptoms similar to what my mother experienced. I had a fibroid growing in me when I thought I was carrying a baby.

I am grateful that the Holy Spirit showed me why I felt rejected all my life.

This lie began with a wrong diagnosis from the doctors. Because of their error, Velma was never considered a person in the womb but a tumor. All her life she suffered with rejection and didn't feel like a person. Life moved on, yet this lie needed to be exposed and destroyed in her life.

The Bible states, "Whosoever shall call on the name of the Lord shall be saved" (Romans 10:13). This salvation encompasses healing and deliverance in every area of life. My wife prayed for Velma and watched Jesus Christ expose this lie that she received before birth. The Holy Spirit, not hypnosis, brought this incident back to her remembrance. (See John 14:26.)

Thomas Verny, M.D., in *The Secret Life of the Unborn Child,* writes, "There is no doubt that core feelings such as love or rejection impinge on the unborn from a very early age."[3] He continues, "In short, then while external stresses a woman faces matter, what matters most is the way she feels about her unborn child. Her thoughts and feelings are the material out of which the unborn child fashions himself."[4]

In Velma's case, her mother had no feelings about her because she was not acknowledged as a baby but a tumor. There were no thoughts and feelings by which she could fashion herself.

Modern medical research has discovered that touching a portion of the brain with a special electrical probe causes a person to emotionally reexperience a situation even if he or she had long forgotten it. "Each patient," Dr. Penfield wrote in his report on the experiments, "does not just remember exact photographic or phonographic reproductions of past scenes and events . . . he feels again the emotions which the situations actually produced in him . . . what he saw and heard and felt and understood." This is why long-forgotten slights, defeats, and conflicts continue to pull at us. Even our most deeply buried memories have emotional resonances, which influence us in perplexing and often troubling ways.[5]

Because the brain has no pain fibers, Dr. Penfield was able to operate on conscious patients. In the course of surgery, he stimulated different parts of the brain with an electrical probe. He learned the brain works like a computer hard drive, which stores information that can be pulled up with the right manipulation or stimulation.

Dr. Verny states, "There is, however, no question that the unborn child remembers or that he retains his memories. It is these long forgotten memories in the unconscious that cause many people in the Body of Christ not to be able to function as they should."

If the doctor can touch off memories with an electrical probe, what can the Holy Spirit do? When we open up to the truth and invoke the healing presence of God, we will begin to experience mighty deliverance and healing.

The lies, distorted images, and symbols must be removed from within so we can be all God has intended us to be. As you continue to read, examine your life. Ask yourself these questions:

1. Do I have recurring situations in my life?

2. Is something going on that I can't seem to control or get rid of?

3. Do I find myself sometimes regressing to a period of time in my childhood?

If you answered yes to any of these questions, you may have some bitter roots that are springing up and causing trouble. If you don't deal with them now, they will eventually defile many (Hebrews 12:15). Be real with yourself and let the Lord bring healing to those areas of your life that keep haunting you.

Let's lay the ax to the root of the past!

The ax already lies at the root of the tree, and the tree that fails to produce good fruit will be cut down and thrown into the fire (Matthew 3:1, Phillips).

As Drs. George and Yvonne Abatso have noted in their book, *How to Equip the African American Family*, "We cannot move ahead until we've looked behind."[6]

Chapter Two

Distorted Images

God gave the Israelites specific instructions as they stood at the threshold of entering the Promised Land. What would ensure their success as they dispossessed these heathen people? After driving out the inhabitants of the land, the Israelites were ordered to destroy all evil influences.

And the Lord spake unto Moses in the plains of Moab by Jordan near Jericho, saying, Speak unto the children of Israel, and say unto them, When ye are passed over Jordan into the land of Canaan; Then ye shall drive out all the inhabitants of the land from before you, and destroy all their pictures, and destroy all their molten images, and quite pluck down all their high places: and ye shall dispossess the inhabitants of the land, and dwell therein: for I have given you the land to possess it (Numbers 33:50-53).

When we are born into this world, our family and environment begin to leave impressions upon our minds. We've seen that these conscious and subconscious impressions can go back as far as the womb, but for now let's focus on the images that shape our minds after birth.

Battleground of the Mind

Scriptures says that as a man "thinketh in his heart, so is he" (Proverbs 23:7). It's no surprise that Satan attacks our minds with such force. If he can win the battle for the mind, he controls our attitudes and actions.

Might we have some pictures, images, or high places in our minds that must be destroyed before we can experience truly liberated lives? God has equipped us to eradicate these enemies by the power of His Spirit.

> For though we walk in the flesh, we do not war after the flesh: (For the weapons of our warfare are not carnal, but mighty through God to the pulling down of strong holds;) Casting down imaginations, and every high thing that exalted itself against the knowledge of God, and bringing into captivity every thought to the obedience of Christ; And having in a readiness to revenge all disobedience, when your obedience is fulfilled (2 Cor. 10:3-6).

These verses clearly show that our warfare is spiritual and psychological. Strongholds in the mind need to be pulled down. The word *stronghold* speaks of a fortress and a prison. The enemy's stronghold in our mind, like a fortress, keeps truth from getting in. The prison in the mind suppresses things that need to be released.

The Bible states, "If our gospel is 'veiled,' the veil must be in the minds of those who are spiritually dying. The spirit of this world has blinded the minds of those who do not believe, and perverts the light of the glorious gospel of Christ, the Image of God, from shining on them" (2 Cor. 4:3, Phillips).

In other words, if the good news (gospel) is veiled or hidden, the veil must be in the minds of those who are spiritually dying. Satan has blinded the minds of those who do not believe. They can't believe because the spirit of this world prevents the light of truth from shining into their minds and exposing the lies and deceptions.

The light that needs to get in is the image of God – the image in which we were originally created. When we're exposed to the light of Christ, the Anointed One, the image of God helps us to develop into God's intended purpose for our lives. This image of God, properly expressed through others, enables me to become the person God intended me to be. Herein lies our problem: All too often we're not exposed to true and right images.

This is why the Lord gave the command to destroy the pictures, molten images, and high places of the enemy that proceed from the spirit of this world.

The word imaginations, from the verse "casting down imaginations" (2 Cor. 10:5), comes from the Greek word *logismos*,[1] from which we derive the word logic. We can see the word *image* in the word imagination. In the warfare for our mind, we must cast down the erroneous images and pictures that we have exalted and served.

Let's examine the word *arguments*, found in the Revised Standard Version of 2 Corinthians 10:5. "We destroy arguments and every proud obstacle to the knowledge of God, and take every thought captive to obey Christ."

The images and pictures impressed upon the mind cause us to argue with ourselves about why we can't do what we should be doing. That's why we can't be ourselves – and the reason many of us even despise ourselves. Arguing with distorted images and pictures of self has kept many wonderful people from becoming what God has purposed for them.

Know, Love, and Accept Yourself

Many people have a wrong attitude about themselves and others. In Leanne Payne's outstanding work, *Restoring the Christian Soul Through Healing Prayer,* she states, "We develop immature, negative patterns of relating to God and others when we've failed to come into a mature self-acceptance."[2] Our inner vision of ourselves is diseased in respect to self-acceptance and the importance of knowing our true selves. You fully recognize that you are a dependent being and you need someone outside of yourself to become. This isn't a self-love that doesn't include God and others. I do believe that persons cannot have mature self-acceptance and self-love without others to affirm them and love them for who they are.

In order for me to love you, I must first love myself (Matthew 22:39). In order for a man to love his wife, he must first have self-love (Ephesians 5:33).

In the same way that the Lord commanded Moses to tear down the high places, the apostle Paul urged the church to cast down every high thing that keeps us from the knowledge of God. Why? As we know God, we will truly know ourselves. Our personhood will also develop through others' affirmation of who we are and should be.

We are not creatures of instinct like other animals. When raised with different species, animals instinctively know who and what they are. They won't get confused by their environment and start acting like some other animal.

But human beings become what they are exposed to. If a child is raised with animals, the child will take on the attributes of the animal. We must be taught to behave humanly. It doesn't happen automatically. In order for a human being to love, love must be expressed by another human being. In order for a human to be affectionate, affection must be received and shown by another.

Leanne Payne writes from an essay by Romano Guardini, Catholic philosopher and theologian, "The act of self-acceptance is the root of all things. I must agree to be the person I am. Agree to have qualifications which I have. Agree to live within the limitations set for me.... The clarity and the courageousness of this acceptance is the foundation of all existence.

"Non-acceptance ranges from the rejection of some physical aspect of our being to a wholesale hatred or rejection of oneself!"[3]

Acceptance of self is the foundation of all existence. This powerful statement is in agreement with the Word of God (Matthew 22:39; Ephesians 5:33). When a person doesn't know himself or accept himself, he has no foundation for his existence.

We depend on others to affirm us as the person God intended us to be. Look back at your family and social environment. How were you parented? What kind of parent have you become? Is our society producing humans or animals?

What's happening in our world is a direct result of our families and social molds. Let's look at the images that formed us.

A Father's Role

God intended the family to be an environment that would eventually lead a child to a greater dependency on Him. The family is responsible for bringing each person into his or her foundation of self-acceptance. But what if you're raised by a family where the members had great difficulty accepting themselves? How can someone who doesn't know who he is help me to lay a foundation for who I am suppose to be?

Nevertheless, God chose the family for this task. In spite of its inherent risks and potential for brokenness, the family has been ordained to form much of our identity. Fathers shoulder much of the responsibility for the character and identity of their children.

The image and picture of manhood is modeled in the man who heads the family. If the man is absent, this is a dysfunctional home. The man is responsible for the family because he was created first and given responsibilities by God. Therefore, any problems in the world, government, society, community, and family must be traced back to the man.

In recent years we have begun to hear more about the importance of men and the father's role in the family. The father, along with the mother, nurtures the children (Ephesians 6:4).

In John and Paula Sanford's book, *Restoring the Christian Family*, the authors state, "Everything a father does in the presence of a son or daughter is an implantation of what the father is to the children. A child does not become what the father says; he becomes what the father is."[4] Even when the child vows not to become like the father, the vow causes the child to be even more like the father or worse. (I recommend John and Paula Sanford's book, *The Transformation of the In-*

ner Man, to fully understand the vows people make and suffer from today.)

Leanne Payne states, "But just as the mother is so vital to these first months and even years (the infant does not know itself to be separate from its mother, and it is in her love and acceptance that it comes to a secure sense of being), so the father is vital in affirming the child's gender identity."[5] The parents don't have the same function in the development of the child. The role of the father during child development is crucial to gender identity.

Homosexual and lesbian behavior is on the rise like never before. Why? Strong, loving, and affirming fathers are not around to declare the child's sexual identity. Without a father's affirmation, a young man will grow up with a distorted image of what manhood is really all about. Young men will impregnate young ladies and not take responsibility for their children. They will seek to have as many young ladies as possible. Without a proper model, young men will not be able to function as true men. God is very concerned with the role of the father today because He knows how vital his role is in the development of the family.

> Behold, I will send you Elijah the prophet before the coming of the great and dreadful day of the Lord: And he shall turn the heart of the fathers to the children, and the heart of the children to their fathers, lest I come and smite the earth with a curse (Malachi 4:5,6).

It's going to take the spirit of Elijah to turn the father's heart and put him back in his position so our future generations won't have the wrong images of masculinity and femininity. The Spirit of Elijah was one of confrontation. We must oppose the wrong images and the twisting of truth to turn the hearts of the father.

The African-American Family

In spite of what many believe, some unique problems plague the African image. In the Church many blacks, as well as whites, say, "It doesn't matter now. We are all one in Christ. There's no color in God. Can't we just move on and get past all this racial stuff?"

This comment sounds spiritual. We look forward to the day when we will not have to address such matters, but today is not the day. For African Americans and African people in general, to continue the way we're going would mean building on a lie.

An old African proverb says, "We cannot move ahead until we've looked behind." Drs. George and Yvonne Abatso share their alarm over the African American family:

> There is a growing underclass in America, containing a high percentage of blacks and minorities, who will never have a full-time job in their lifetimes. Think of the impact the condition alone will have on black family life.
>
> At least 44 percent of black families are headed by females, compared to 13 percent for white households. Seventy-five percent of black children under six are raised in poverty. The average black child can expect to spend more than five years of his childhood in poverty as compared to ten months for the average white child....
>
> When looking at the African-American family, it's not difficult to see that something is seriously wrong. *The family is critical to the survival of a people.*[6]

If we don't wake up from our sleep as a people, the freedom that we thought we had will cease to exist, and our hope of overcoming will become a faded dream of the past.

My first book, *The Roots of Deliverance,* mentions how Jesus and the apostle Paul desired their own race to be saved. The Bible states, "He came unto his own, and his own received him not" (John 1:11). Jesus came to minister and to reach His own race with the gospel. Jesus sent forth the 12 disciples, saying, "Go not into the way of the Gentiles, and into any city of the Samaritans enter ye not: But go rather to the lost sheep of the house of Israel" (Matthew 10:5,6).

The apostle Paul said, "For I could wish that I myself were cursed and cut off from Christ for the sake of my brothers, those of my own race, the people of Israel" (Romans 9:3, NIV). When a black man begins to reach out to his people, he's referred to as a racist and anti-white. If you're going to label as racist anyone who reaches out to his own community, you must also put Jesus and the apostle Paul in the same category. They wanted to see their own race touched and changed by the power of the gospel.

When Africans arrived in America, the destruction of a people with a rich heritage continued. I won't spend a lot of time looking back at the terrible events of slavery, but I will concentrate on the distorted images and pictures that have been projected and introjected into the minds of African people.

African Americans suffer from an identity crisis. Many of us don't know and don't understand who we are. If we don't learn some lessons from the past, we are destined to repeat them.

Professor Amos N. Wilson writes, "Blacks suffer from a slave mentality, which is the result of the most massive and successful behavioral modification and brainwashing program in history."[7]

Yet most of our church and political leaders won't tell the whole truth. Partial truth makes a people only partially free!

We must explain to African Americans exactly what took place in their mentality. They need to be deprogrammed in order to be reprogrammed that they might begin to flow in God's program for their lives and take their God intended place in the Body of Christ.

The Media Image

Media is derived from the Latin word *medius*, which means mid or middle. Control is defined as the condition of being directed or restrained; restraint. The media can control the direction of our mental perception.[8]

Television plays a major role in the mental perception of ourselves as African Americans. We look at different programs to be entertained, yet our image is being marred as we view black actors who have sold out to the dollar bill. Money seems to mean more than self-respect and self-love. Programs such as "In Living Color" have black men dressing and looking like females. That in itself is disgraceful, but they also make the female dancers look like prostitutes, degrading the women of our culture.

"The Wayans Brothers" is another new program that continues to place us back on the plantation as clowns, trying to keep the master entertained.

When I visit my old neighborhood in Watts, I see billboards with black men holding guns surrounded by beautiful women of color. Our sisters look sexy with a bottle of Black Velvet liquor in their hands.

Slavemasters in the U.S. had captives from Africa picking tobacco leaves; now billboards in black communities send deceptive messages of how cool you can be by smoking Kools.

Na'im Akbar writes in his book, *Chains & Images of Psychological Slavery,* "The limited number of powerful and dignified images of African Americans in the media and the community as a whole reduces our sense of self-respect. This is a continuation of the slavery patterns. Only those persons who looked liked, acted like, and thought in the framework or reference of the master were completely acceptable."[9]

What would happen if black actors refused to act until roles were given to uplift the black community? Many of our people are in positions to help bring about positive change in our communities. Unfortunately, too many have chosen to remain silent as to what's important. They make speeches to appear as if they really care. African Americans must get in touch with who they were before the American experience. Let's connect with our past so we can bring healing to our present and change our future.

Projection and Introjection

Earlier in this chapter I mentioned the word *projection.* What does it mean? "The standard textbook definition of ego defensive projection refers to . . . the means by which the ego disavows or refuses to recognize its own discreditable traits and self-incriminating motives by attributing those traits and motives to others."[10]

Have you ever wondered why someone writes a book or devises a new study in an attempt to prove the inferiority of the black mind? When someone constantly tries to prove his superiority, he is really feeling the pressures of his own inferiority. Whenever people try to put you in a particular category, ask yourself, "Why are they doing this and who will benefit from such deceptive information?"

I have a radio broadcast that reaches into the state prison in Lancaster, CA. My program tells the predominately black population of inmates that how they are viewed by others has caused them to view themselves in the same manner. What has been true about others was *projected* onto the African-American male in particular.

To *introject* is to "incorporate unconsciously into the psyche (a mental image of an object, person, etc.) and focus aggressive energy upon this image rather than the object itself."[11]

Amos Wilson writes, "The introjection of eurocentrically falsified African images into the collective African-American personality can only occur when African Americans themselves accept those falsified images as fact."[12]

It's satanic for Euro-Americans to introject these false images onto others. But what's worse is the acceptance of this lie as truth.

Wilson continues, "This acceptance of false images by African Americans is made all the more easy and efficient by the fact that information, whether true or untrue, is almost completely controlled and manipulated by white American academic and propaganda establishments."[13] Because of this control and manipulation of information, we must seek out information from within our culture from men and women who will express truth without compromise.

The Image of the Son of God

Scripture forbids making the likeness of anything that is in heaven, earth, or under the earth. That means making visual images or pictures of the Son of God is against the written Word of God.

Thou shalt not make unto thee any graven image, or any likeness of any thing that is in heaven above, or that is in the earth beneath, or that is in the water under the earth (Exodus 20:4).

Despite the clear command of Scripture, men insisted on painting the likeness of Christ. These portraits should never have been painted. To make matters worse, most paintings are historically and biblically incorrect. But there is a reason for this wrong and distorted image of the Son of God.

Dr. Frances Cress Welsing, in *The Isis Papers*, reveals the motive for this distortion:

Absolutely critical to the white supremacy system of religious thought was the formation of the image of a white man as the Son of God. Because the brain-computer functions most fundamentally on logic circuits, at deep unconscious levels it automatically computes that God, the Father, is also a white male. If God is other than white, scientifically, He would have produced a black (or other non-white) Son.

With this unconscious logic circuit of "God is white" firmly in place, white domination over non-white people could last for one trillion years. With the white man as God, the nonwhite global collective would be obedient to the white man always.[14]

Na'im Akbar concurs with this thought: "Once you begin to believe that the deity is somebody other than you, then you are put into a psychologically dependent state that renders you incapable of breaking loose until you break the hold of that image."[15]

When Europeans began to explore the world, they discovered that the majority of the world's population was and is non-white. Napoleon ordered his soldiers to disfigure the statues and bodies that lay in the tombs of Egypt. Why? So no one would be able to recognize that these great contributors and inventors were black people. Instead of appreciating the contributions made by the Africans in the land of Ham, Europeans felt insecure and inferior and set out to project what they felt about themselves onto non-whites all over the world.

Is it any wonder that the highest deity that men can look to is in the image of someone other than themselves?

When a person is insecure about who he is and what he can accomplish, he must find security in stepping on others so that he can feel important. Notice I said *feel* important. In reality he feels like he is not important and must degrade others to gain a sense of importance.[16]

Because of their need to be important and have meaning in life, those who felt inferior to the rest of the world's population made the highest deity of all in their own image.

Even on Christian television someone claimed to have had a vision of a white-skinned Jesus. Over the past decade it has been discovered that Jesus could not have been white living where He did. The whites now living in Africa have descended from Europeans who migrated there for the purpose of controlling the world's richest continent in natural resources. Their mission may have been accomplished, but God's plan will prevail!

Descendants of Africa must first remove these lying images from their homes and churches. Why? We paint the wrong image in the minds of our children and teach them that whites are superior.

We need an anointing to break down the images of this historically incorrect portrait. The Word of God implies that in order to bring forth good treasure, we must have previously deposited good treasure in our storehouse (Matthew

12:35). Let's replace these distorted images with biblical, historical truth. We can reverse what has happened to our minds through lies and deceptions.

Chapter Three

Psychological Death

Most of us have heard a sermon preached on the vision of the valley of dry bones. Ministers often use Ezekiel 37 in an effort to wake-up spiritually dead souls in their congregation, often with little or no lasting results.

Part of the problem with such a sermon is it has been preached void of a message. Anyone can attend seminary and learn, through homiletics and hermeneutics, how to prepare and deliver a good sermon. All too often, however, ministers lack a message from the Messenger Himself.

There is a difference between a well-prepared sermon and a cutting-edge message!

Let's look at the message of the prophet Ezekiel.

The hand of the Lord was upon me, and carried me out in the spirit of the Lord, and set me down in the midst of the valley which was full of bones, and caused me to pass by them round about: and, behold, there were very many in the open valley; and, lo, they were very dry.

And he said unto me, Son of man, can these bones live? And I answered, O Lord God, thou knowest. Again he said unto me, Prophesy upon these bones, and say unto them, O ye dry bones, hear the word of the Lord. Thus saith the Lord God unto these bones; Behold, I will cause breath to enter into you, and ye shall live: And I will lay sinews upon you, and will bring up flesh upon you, and cover you with skin, and put breath in you, and ye shall live; and ye shall know that I am the Lord.

So I prophesied as I was commanded: and as I prophesied, there was a noise, and behold a shaking, and the bones came together, bone to its bone. And when I beheld, lo, the sinews and the flesh came up upon them, and the skin covered them above: but there was no breath in them. Then said he unto me, Prophesy unto the wind, prophesy, son of man, and say to the wind, Thus saith the Lord God; Come from the four winds, O breath, and breathe upon these slain, that they may live.

So I prophesied as he commanded me, and the breath came into them, and they lived, and stood up upon their feet, an exceeding great army. Then he said unto me, Son of man, these bones are the whole house of Israel: behold, they say, Our bones are dried, and our hope is lost: we are cut off for our parts.

Therefore prophesy and say unto them, Thus saith the Lord God; Behold, O my people, I will open your graves, and cause you to come up out of your graves, and bring you into the land of Israel. And ye shall know that I am the Lord, when I have opened your graves, O my people, and brought you up out of your graves, and shall put my spirit in you, and ye shall live, and I shall place you in your own land: then shall ye know that I the Lord have spoken it, and performed it, saith the Lord (Ezekiel 37:1-14).

Ezekiel was carried out in the Spirit of the Lord, set down in a valley of very dry bones, and given a word of prophecy.

Speaking Life to the Dead

The Lord asked the prophet, "Can these bones live?" God didn't pose this question because He didn't know the answer. God showed Ezekiel the death that had come upon a people and the hopeless fate that had befallen them. There was no way for death to produce life. God Himself had to breathe life into this great army.

The life came by the word of the Lord. Years later the word of the Lord would say, "Lazarus, come forth." Only God can bring life out of death because He defeated death, hell, and the grave (Hebrews 2:14,15). After Ezekiel prophesied the word of the Lord to the dead bones, breath (the life of God) came upon these slain that they might live. When God speaks, His Spirit moves to bring the manifestation of what He said.

And they went forth, and preached every where, the Lord working with them, and confirming the word with signs following (Mark 16:20).

When the Lord is working *with* you, He will confirm His Word with signs following. That's why we need a message from the Lord working within us and not a sermon that we worked up.

This is why we are not experiencing the move of God that other countries have seen. People who say they are receiving words from the Lord are not – because the Lord confirms *His* word, not *our* word. The word of the Lord, along with His Spirit (breath), is being spoken to a people who are dead.

Ezekiel 37:11 says, "Our bones are dried, and our hope is lost: we are cut off for our parts."

I believe this is a very accurate description of African people born in America.

Mental Paralysis

Not only have we been completely cut off from our land, but we have also been cut off from being ourselves and thinking independently. Amos Wilson states, "Enslavement of black people was not just physical but more importantly it was mental."[1]

Black people have been unconsciously paralyzed. It's as if they've been affected by narcosis, defined as "a condition of deep stupor which passes into unconsciousness and paralysis."[2] When you paralyze a person's mind, it brings the mind into a condition of helpless inactivity. The mind becomes ineffective and powerless.

We have become incapable of making decisions for ourselves that will benefit us as a race of people. When blacks arrived here from Africa, the land of Ham, they were taught from birth that thinking independently was not something they should be inspired to do. If one dared to think from within, rather than from what he was told by his master, a slave was punished and sometimes even killed.

Dr. Carter G. Woodson, in his work, *The Miseducation of the Negro,* makes some telling statements concerning the potential of our race:

The Negro will never be able to show all his originality as long as his efforts are directed from without by those who socially proscribe him.[3]

What Negroes are now being taught does not bring their minds into harmony with life as they must face it.[4]

African-American people are trapped by unconscious programming and are still doing what they are told without preparing to go beyond the limits that white America has set for them. When we begin to look at the mind of African people in America, we can begin to understand why many have great difficulty receiving the truth about who they are in relation to historical and biblical truth. The conditioning of the mind psychodynamically has caused such a deep paralysis many believe that they're all right when in reality they are asleep!

Psychological death sets in when someone else's opinion or stereotype of you becomes your reality.

We as a people must begin to realize that we are not what we have become! We are much more than what we have become.

The bondage in the mind of African people runs deep. But our God has spoken, "Behold, O my people, I will open your graves, . . ." (Ezekiel 37:12). "Princes shall come out of Egypt; Ethiopia shall soon stretch out her hands unto God" (Psalms 68:31).

Walking in the Natural

God revealed a prophetic principle in 1 Corinthians 15:42-49, which is "first the natural, then the spiritual." In reality, it's a principle of restoration. Before the fall of man, we know that the "worlds were framed by the word of God, so that things which are seen were not made of things which do appear" (Hebrews 11:3). So we know that it all came out of the Spirit. But in the process of restoration, the principle becomes reversed: "First the natural, then the spiritual."[5]

The Word of God admonishes us to "walk in the Spirit, and ye shall not fulfil the lust of the flesh" (Galatians 5:16). But the walk in the Spirit can't be done effectively without some practical things being first walked out in the natural realm. Walking in the Spirit is quite difficult for many believers because they haven't mastered walking in the natural yet!

Based on my experience with the people of God, many church leaders have tried in vain to get people to walk in the Spirit before bringing healing and correction to the natural man. Our spiritual walk will ultimately be affected by our past natural foundations. For this reason, we must relay foundations in the natural in order to walk effectively in the Spirit.

I am not referring to our initial salvation experience but sanctification after salvation. F. Earle Fox writes, "Sanctification is simply an extension of the original gift of salvation. It is the bringing under submission to God of those parts of ourselves that cannot or will not respond to the normal conscious spiritual discipline."[6] In 1 Thessalonians 5:23 the apostle Paul prays, "and the very God of peace *sanctify you wholly;* and I pray God your *whole* spirit and soul and body be preserved blameless unto the coming of our Lord Jesus Christ."

The apostle Paul wrote to that church, showing them the need for sanctification after salvation. He also wrote the church at Corinth, "Having therefore these promises, dearly beloved, let us cleanse ourselves from all filthiness of the flesh and spirit, perfecting holiness in the fear God" (2 Corinthians 7:1).

I believe the Church has not done an adequate job in bringing the people of God into the wholeness that's available to every believer.

When Jesus met a man who had an infirmity for eight years, He asked him a question. "When Jesus saw him lie, and knew that he had been now a long time in that case, he saith unto him, Wilt thou be made whole?" (John 5:6). Many of God's people have been afflicted with spiritual paralysis, unable to move on with their lives after salvation. I pose these questions to you: Are you saved and still in bondage? What were you saved from? Do you want to be made whole?

We preach to people about heaven to take their minds off their condition on earth. We fail to realize that God wants us to have an abundant life here on earth as well. It starts with us being whole in spirit, soul, and body.

> Jesus saith unto him, Rise, take up thy bed, and walk. And immediately the man was made whole, and took up his bed, and walked: and on the same day was the sabbath (John 5:8,9).

When we become whole, we will carry the thing that once carried us! Those things that physically and psychologically bound us will cease being when we allow Jesus to make us whole.

The Enslavement of the Mind

Just how important is our thinking? Dr. Carter G. Woodson affirms that our thought life determines our behavior. In his writing he states:

> If you can control a man's thinking, you do not have to worry about his action. When you determine what a man shall think, you do not have to concern yourself about what he will do. If you make a man feel that he is inferior, you do not have to compel him to accept an inferior status, for he will seek it himself. If you make a man think that he is justly an outcast, you do not have to order him to the back door. He will go

without being told; and if there is no back door, his very nature will demand one.[7]

Dr. Woodson, in *The Miseducation of the Negro*, has eloquently written about the African's desire to want freedom if knowledge was allowed to enter his mind. Many of the plantation owners believed that keeping the African ignorant and mentally enslaved would keep him from desiring to be free from his control. I don't think African people really know the depth of bondage and death that has been projected and introjected in their minds. The fact that we can't come together to the degree that we should, should show us that something is definitely wrong with our thinking concerning each other.

We must remember that before our American experience we did not have the problem of disunity among ourselves. In order to correct many of the bondages within our race, we must first rediscover who we were before our forced captivity in America. We need to look at Africa and other countries where non-whites were exploited.

The apostle Paul wrote, "And be renewed in the spirit of your mind" (Ephesians 4:23). Whenever a word begins with the prefix *re*, it means back, returning to a previous state. To renew the spirit of the mind doesn't mean get a new mind. But we must go back to a previous state of mind that we once had. In other words, we must return to the way we once thought of ourselves.

Our minds have a spirit. According to *Vine's Expository Dictionary of New Testament Words*, the word spirit in Ephesians 4:23 carries the meaning of purpose, aim. We must be renewed in the purpose or aim of our mind. We must reevaluate how our minds have been conditioned and what we are aiming at.

I must ask myself these questions: What should control me? How do I feel or what do I know to be true?[8] I may feel insignificant and inferior, but is that the truth?

As we work to bring our minds out of enslavement, we must be able to separate our feelings about ourselves from what is really true about ourselves. Scripture affirms that we have been created in the very image and likeness of God:

> And God said, Let us make man in our image, after our likeness: and let them have dominion over the fish of the sea, and over the fowl of the air, and over the cattle, and over all the earth, and over every creeping thing that creepeth upon the earth (Genesis 1:26).

I mentioned earlier that Euro-Americans have made a man (people) after their own image and likeness. Men have taken control of the minds of other men through lies and deceptions. After all this psychological damage has been inflicted on successive generations of African Americans, many are saying, "Hey, get over it. That was a long time ago." But when you live with it and must deal with it in the lives of your people, it becomes a driving force that won't stop until the mission is accomplished. I refuse to leave African minds in such a destructive, preprogrammed mind-set when God has given me knowledge to deprogram and reprogram our minds in order to get in God's program for proper identity. We must recognize that the first man, Adam, was created in Africa in the image and likeness of God (Genesis 2:7-14).

Self-Hatred

How could this African man, created in the image and likeness of God, end up hating his own image many years later?

Amos Wilson contends, "It is well-known that the black man suffers from self-hatred as a result of his American experience. One of the symptoms of this self-hatred is a strong wish to deny in various ways their blackness which they see as the source of their inferiority and the source of their degradation by whites."[9]

In order to make a man a slave, you must first convince him that he should be one.

In my first book, *The Roots of Deliverance,* I looked at the so-called curse on the black race where Noah said, "Cursed be Canaan; a servant of servants shall he be unto his brethren" (Genesis 9:25). These words fell on Ham's youngest son, or Noah's grandson.

European Americans used the Bible to convince Africans that they were a race of cursed people on whom God had completely turned His back and even despised.

Wayne Perryman's book, *The 1993 Trial on the Curse of Ham,* shows how Christian publications have continued to spread the lie that African people and their descendants are a cursed people. These publications have no understanding of Genesis 9:20-27, yet they continue to hold fast to lies in an effort to feel justified in their mistreatment of African people and their descendants.

In order to mistreat someone, you must put him in a category that will permit mental justification of his mistreatment. Euro-Americans have sub-humanized African people. When a race is viewed as less than human, the one with that view can then feel justified in any treatment of that race.

When a black man is beaten in the streets, as we saw with Rodney King, the police feel justified in their actions because of their view of black people, especially black men. Unfortunately, blacks have allowed the distorted views that others have of us to become projected onto us and internalized.

Amos Wilson, in his work entitled *Black on Black Violence,* discussed the self-contempt that black men have for self and others of the same race:

> The black-on-black violent criminal hates in other blacks those characteristics he hates most in himself. His expressed contempt for and attacks on other blacks are the means by which he refrains from recognizing and expressing his self-contempt. By externalizing his self-contempt he stays his own hand from attacking himself. He commits homicide to keep from committing suicide. His homicidal mania, violent rages, are curious and/or perverted forms of self-preservation.[10]

He commits homicide to prevent from committing suicide, which promotes the genocide of our people. When black men are convinced that they are sub-human, they act according to the lie they have received about themselves.

Along with the distortion of Scripture and the internalizing of false images, our families have contributed largely to the lying images we now hold of ourselves. When a child doesn't receive the nurturing, love, and sense of being from parents, this causes the child to be persuaded early that he or she is insignificant and doesn't have a secure place in this world. This will definitely add to the self-hatred of anyone not receiving proper affirmation and love from the ones who were suppose to give it.

Self-hatred causes a person to reach out and attack others in an effort to preserve his own life. When I kill my brother, I'm actually killing myself, but I kill my brother because I'm afraid to physically kill myself. What we must do is teach our brothers how to love themselves, and the power of love will stop the senseless killing of our people. Only the unconditional love of God can turn self-hatred into a love and respect for self.

We need to embrace the truth that the psalmist penned thousands of years ago. He stood in awe of his own creation. "I will praise thee; for I am fearfully and wonderfully made: marvellous are thy works; and that my soul knoweth right well" (Psalm 139:14).

We must speak the truth, let the truth speak for itself, and make no apologies for the truth that has been spoken!

Inferiority

What does Scripture say about race and inferiority? God showed the apostle Peter that He did not favor Jews by pouring out the Holy Spirit on Gentiles when the apostle preached to Cornelius' household. Peter remarked, "Of a truth I perceive that God is no respecter of persons" (Acts 10:34). Scripture also says this:

> Lo, mine eye hath seen all this, mine ear hath heard and understood it. What ye know, the same do I know also: I am not inferior unto you (Job 13:1,2).

Dr. Mensa Otabil, in his book, *Beyond the Rivers of Ethiopia*, explains what it takes to make a person inferior.

> Inferiority is developed when you do not see what someone else sees, hear what he hears, understand what he understands, or know what he knows. So then if any individual or group of people meant to dominate you, they would endeavor to manipulate what you see, hear, and understand.

> That has been the method used by all oppressive human institutions, be they governments, religious organizations, or corporations. That is why the media represents the most potent force for either the control or the liberation of a people. When someone controls what you see, hear, understand, and know, he can make you feel inferior about yourself and develop a sense of self-hatred and alienation.

What we see, hear, understand, and know has been so tightly controlled that when you grow up, you could spend all your life unconsciously trying to be like somebody else. With this condition, why would you not feel inferior about yourself![11]

Upon arriving in America, Africans saw, heard, and experienced many things to put and keep them in a state of feeling inferior. To be inferior, according to *Webster's New World Edition Dictionary*, is to be low, below, under, or subordinate. If I look at you as a man of my equal, I cannot consciously treat you in any other manner than a man of my equal.

To help justify their deeds and ease their guilt, Euro-Americans had to look on us as inferior to treat us like beasts of burden. Africans were of a different culture but not inferior. Our differences, however, were used against us. We were made to believe that being different meant being superior or inferior.

In 1712, Willie Lynch addressed the plantation owners in Virginia and told them that he had a foolproof plan to keep black people in bondage for hundreds, perhaps thousands, of years. He stated, "I have outlined a number of differences among the slaves; and I take these differences and make them bigger. I use fear, distrust, and envy for control purposes."[12]

Differences among our race were used to create divisions among us that are still in effect today! Willie Lynch continues, "The black slave after receiving this indoctrination shall carry and will become self-refueling and self-generating for hundreds of years, maybe thousands."

That's why I'm writing this book. Our people don't even realize the degree of precalculated damage that enslaves and cripples our minds today that was perpetuated through the demonic institution of slavery. Mental chains are not unlocked through legislation but through the power of truth and the Spirit of God to heal and restore.

One of the differences used among blacks was skin color. Darker skinned blacks were looked upon as the lower one of the race.

My grandmother told me how her aunt questioned the girls about the skin color of their dates. She asked them, "Is he a black nigger?" My grandmother said they were encouraged to marry someone with a lighter complexion. As I stated earlier, dark skin was seen as a curse based on the distortion of Scripture and the differences placed between us for control purposes.

When I was about 14 years old, I had a girlfriend whose complexion was much lighter than mine. Once we got into an argument, and in her anger she said, "Black nigger!" Throughout school, I can remember those of lighter complexion believing and acting like they were better than their darker brothers and sisters.

The deep brainwashing that our people underwent during their captivity must be reversed! One of our greatest enemies is disunity. That's because in our ignorance we trusted the smiling faces of those used by Satan. We allowed false images, distortions, and lies to enter our minds. The truth, however, lies in Scripture: "I am not inferior unto you" (Job 13:2).

Chapter Four

Searching for Truth

Throughout my years of reading and studying material from many different authors, I have yet to come across any extensive biblical solutions to the deep psychological damage that has afflicted the African mind. Many great writers of African descent, through their presentations of truth, have sought to free the African mind from its mental slavery. No matter how our approaches vary, we agree on this point: My colleagues and I long to see the complete liberation of the African mind from false images.

The first three chapters showed us that some serious issues need to be brought into the light of truth. Many who have read those chapters have already drawn conclusions without examining the whole matter. Remember that prejudice is defined as "a judgment or opinion formed before the facts are known; preconceived idea; to prejudge."[1]

I trust you are not guilty of prejudice based on these first few chapters. When truth begins to surface, like anything that has been suppressed, a lot of discomfort accompanies it. In counseling I have seen the pain that people experience when it's time to bring healing to an area of their life that was traumatized years ago.

When you have been traumatized by longstanding lies, truth operates the same way.

Those who have a genetic connection to the group that was responsible for these lies may begin to feel hurt and pain, along with anger and perhaps some hate, for what is being said – in this case, the truth.

A Warning to Oppressors

People can't do whatever they want and think there are no consequences for their actions. What goes around, comes around. Scripture declares that what we sow, we will also reap (Galatians 6:7).

Now listen, you rich people, weep and wail because of the misery that is coming upon you. Your wealth has rotted, and moths have eaten your clothes. Your gold and silver are corroded. Their corrosion will testify against you and eat your flesh like fire. You have hoarded wealth in the last days. Look! The wages you failed to pay the workmen who mowed your fields are crying out against you. The cries of the harvesters have reached the ears of the Lord Almighty. You have lived on earth in luxury and self-indulgence. You have fattened yourselves in the day of slaughter (James 5:1-5, NIV).

This warning to rich oppressors need to be heeded, and repentance must take place.

America is now reaping what she has sown to build this country.

You can't exploit, lie, and take from another what's not yours and think God will just look the other way and say, "Oh well, that's life."

Europeans will reap the consequences for mistreating God's people all over the world.

How Should We Respond?

Our job as black people is to be patient and in our patience remove the mental injustices by embracing historical and biblical truth. We should allow our history to do more for us than give us a sense of pride every February during Black History Month while remaining content with our past accomplishments and contributions to the world. We must learn from our mistakes and develop solutions to regain power in our lives.

As we strive for mastery, we must cry out against all lies and transfer knowledge to the next generation.

> Don't have anything to do with foolish and stupid arguments, because you know they produce quarrels. And the Lord's servant must not quarrel; instead, he must be kind to everyone, able to teach, not resentful. Those who oppose him he must gently instruct, in the hope that God will grant them repentance leading them to a knowledge of the truth, and that they will come to their senses and escape from the trap of the devil, who has taken them captive to do his will (2 Timothy 2:23-25, NIV).

We are not to quarrel and get involved in arguments about the truth. We are to instruct with the hope that the oppressors of black people will repent and come to their senses and escape the trap by which they have been snared.

Conforming to Truth

Let's examine the mental and emotional processes underlying human behavior and its motivation, especially as developed unconsciously in response to environmental influences, which is known as psychodynamics.

Many bondages have captured the minds of black people, and much of the destruction was accomplished through unconscious programming. Not being aware of these things, we allowed ourselves to be taken captive. What we must do now is deprogram and remove distorted images and lies from the deep recesses of our unconscious minds.

Reverend F. Earle Fox writes:

> The healing of the unconscious area of our lives involves feeding good spiritual food into ourselves which indirectly brings about and supports a healthy unconscious. I cannot directly feed the unconscious as I can feed my conscious mind, precisely because it is unconscious. But I can do things which will send good food down into the unconscious level and gradually bring about a transformation of the unconscious levels, freeing me from the bondages which have accrued there.[2]

First of all I must establish a basis for truth and reality as we stated earlier, using the example of the flat table. You must determine what truth and reality are before you can make a conscious effort to receive them. When you look at the world and its inhabitants, God and His Word are the only basis of truth we have.

That means whatever the truth says about my situation, I must receive it and accept it, knowing all truth comes from God. Reverend Fox continues:

The actual feeding is largely a conscious process, the conscious taking authority over the unconscious by feeding godly images down into the spiritual digestive system. The basic images of our mind need to be washed and cleansed to conform to the truth.

When images not of God begin to dominate our conscious or unconscious, however, then we become made in the image of something other than God. We get a case of spiritual indigestion, and sooner or later experience an identity crisis. We have trouble knowing who we are. Until we feed into ourselves the good spiritual food from God, we will never resolve the question of who we are or even whether we can be at all.[3]

The many distortions of who we are can't be removed until we conform to the truth – the truth of who God said we are and not the lying images that have made us believe something other than what God said.

The lies will continue to fight to keep their position over truth, but you must allow the truth to prevail at all costs when it's presented (2 Corinthians 10:4,5).

Removing Distorted Images

Jesus Christ is the Truth. Following Jesus, therefore, is a journey out of the myriad of lies and into truth. Many Africans must also receive a proper image of who Jesus Christ is. Dr. Kunjufu writes:

There have been two lines of thought to counter the European image of Jesus. First, to provide an image of Jesus with African features and what is referred to in the Bible as "woolly hair and feet the color of bronze." And second, to discard the image of Jesus and focus on His works and beliefs. My optimal desire would be the second, because I have no need to express my insecurity by making every image the reflection of myself. The potential problem with no image is that the most recent image may become permanent.[4]

I agree with Dr. Kunjufu to focus on the works and beliefs of Jesus. Focusing on the truth that Jesus taught is far more valuable to us than any painting could ever be.

Dr. Kunjufu mentions the potential problem with no image because of the effects the most recent image has had on our minds.

I have placed a beautiful portrait in our home that depicts Jesus as an African. My purpose is not to express insecurities, but to carefully erase the lie from the minds of my family members. This is a deprogramming process for the purpose of programming with truth.

I am careful to teach my family the value and worth of all men regardless of race. I don't want us to become what others have become. We must constantly remind ourselves that they are not our teachers; God is. Everyone must do what he or she is persuaded to do in his or her own mind (Romans 14:5). The motive of the heart must be in line with the truth.

A difference exists between truth and what is true, however. It is true that many wrongs were done to Africans all over the world, but truth (the revelation of Jesus Christ) causes us to respond in an appropriate manner.

African people must respond by consciously receiving the truth about who they are and not holding bitterness and unforgiveness for what was done.

"God is a Spirit: and they that worship him must worship him in spirit and in truth" (John 4:24).

The spirit of a man who has been regenerated can receive the truth with gladness. But the flesh, or our carnal, worldly nature, will fight to cling to what is not truth. When you begin to get angry in the presence of biblical or historical truth, this is a sign that your flesh is at war with your spirit (Galatians 5:17). Those lies and distorted images of yourself must be released to God in exchange for who He has declared you to be.

As you begin to let God expose the lies and distorted images of yourself, let the truth prevail regardless of how much it hurts. Be honest with yourself about what you have become and then the transformation of the real you can begin. Whether black, white, or any other race, we are in need of transformation by the power of truth.

Security and Significance

Dr. Larry Crabb, in his book, *Effective Biblical Counseling,* describes a basic need that all of us have.

> People have one basic personal need which requires two kinds of inputs for its satisfaction. The most basic need is a sense of personal worth, an acceptance of oneself as a whole, real person. The two required inputs are *significance* (purpose, importance, adequacy for a job, meaningfulness, impact) and *security* (love – unconditional and consistently expressed; permanent acceptance).[5]

In my first book, *The Roots of Deliverance,* I spoke about the need to be recognized as someone important. This is a legitimate need that every human being has. The person who is deprived of a sense of personal worth will seek wrong methods to have this need met in their lives.

People believe that *doing* causes them to *be.* It's so easy for people to look to wrong beliefs to make them worth something.

Before I started teaching black people about who they are and were before their American experience, one of the young sisters in the ministry had a secret desire to be white. She could not see the benefit of being black in America. All she had ever seen was the mistreatment of black people, their struggles to survive, and the white culture's perception of beauty, so she did not want to be a part of the race into which she was born.

I'm sure this young black sister is not alone in her secret desire to be someone other than herself.

The family's role in the development of personal worth and security in a person is very vital to the development of that person as a person. Another testimony of one of our daughters in the ministry clearly expresses the essential role that family plays in the development of a person:

> I was born in the midwest in the mid-1960s. Because my father was in the military, our family traveled a lot. My mother and father were married as teenagers and divorced by the time I was a year old.
>
> Even though my parents divorced as very good friends, I experienced a lot of emotional trauma. When I was conceived and in the womb, my parents were not yet married. My mother was 18 years old, and this was her second pregnancy. My mother told my father that she did not want to have me and desired an abortion. Having two children at such a young age was too much for her. (I didn't learn this until after my salvation.) My father rejected her request for an abortion, and my parents were soon married. After the divorce, my brother and I went to live with my mother.
>
> As a little girl, I had numerous crying spells. If I had any inclination that my mother was disappointed or angry with me, I would cry. This baffled my mother. I always replied that I felt

as if no one loved me nor wanted me around. I always took walks alone and climbed trees – anything to avoid being rejected by people. My closest friend for years was my older brother.

When I was eight years old and in third grade, I attended a predominately white elementary school in Upstate New York for half the school year. My brother and I were a part of the two percent of blacks in the school, which included the teachers. At this point in my life, I was in the care of my father, even though I lived with my grandmother.

Beginning with the first day of school, I was frequently referred to as "nigger." Students made it very clear that I was not welcomed at this particular school. Ironically, my teacher was black. I did not understand why she allowed the other students to call me "nigger" or why she didn't reprimand them for treating me as an outcast. Whether my teacher had actually heard anyone call me "nigger," I don't know; but she had to realize that something was going on.

I remember taking a 100-problem multiplication test in this class. We had approximately 40 minutes to complete the exam. Being skilled in math, especially throughout elementary school and junior high, I finished the exam in about five minutes.

When I handed in my test, the other students (who were all white) looked at each other in awe. My teacher graded my exam and looked at me with surprise, saying, "You got 100 percent on this test." I simply replied, "Okay." Unfortunately, I felt because I was black that I was not suppose to be smarter than white people.

The next year, I returned to live with my mother. This community was the opposite: 98 percent black. When I went to school, I was rejected among my own race because I got good grades. No one wanted to hang out with me because to them

I was the teacher's pet. Consequently, my grades dropped considerably because acceptance meant more to me than good grades.

The impact of being rejected by white people for being black and by black people for being intelligent was enough to cause me to be a good student the rest of my school years – but not the exceptional student I know that I was. At age eight or nine, I desired to be white, but I was never taught why I should desire to be black. Therefore, I began to hate white people for mistreating blacks. I believed that they caused us to hate ourselves.

When I reached junior high, I discovered that all white people did not hate black people, but many still resented my race. A few of my friends were white, but I still did not have a friend to understand and appreciate me as an intelligent, black female.

I remember asking my mother, "How come I'm not white?" Shocked at my question, she asked, "Why do you want to be white?" "White people get treated better," I replied.

My mother did her best to encourage me not to desire to be white. At my young age, however, I wanted someone to explain why I should be proud to be black. My black associates in junior high did not want to be friends with me if I continued to socialize with whites. I was emotionally tired of all these attitudes.

At age 13, I realized that my problem was not that I did not understand my own self. I liked myself, but I wanted others to like me too. I grew tired of trying to prove what I was or wasn't by others' expectations. So I began to be a loner.

By nine years of age, I had gotten into gang activity and drug usage. At home, I was not abused. My mother showed me a lot of affection. Our needs for food and clothing were always met, but my mother's work schedule made it difficult to look after two children. I spent every weekend with my mother but perceived this as not being wanted, therefore I turned to gang activity and drug use.

The next year, my brother and I went to live with my father. I was very obedient, yet sneaky. I moved because my life had been threatened. If I hadn't moved, I would have been killed. I remained with my father until going on my own.

I was surrounded by pornography, drugs, and parties. I was allowed into clubs at an early age and began to make my own decisions as long as I was "true to myself." My father was very attached to me. It was as though he found peace of mind only when he was with me. His emotional attachment began to be expressed sexually, and I lost my virginity at age ten.

My father assured me that our intimate relationship was okay because it was all done in the name of love. This relationship, he told me, was a secret. As a little girl, I wondered if it was special, why did it have to be kept a secret?

I had thought that all girls probably had this kind of relationship with their fathers until I began high school. Being around other teenage girls, I learned that the relationship I had with my father was not common. I subconsciously began to hate my father and suppressed the memories of our intimacy until I came to know Christ. I never told anyone about my relationship with my father. Frankly, it became easier to forget as I got older.

From this time until age 18, I was molested repeatedly by men within and outside my family. Because I had the relationship with my father, again I viewed this as normal. I began to feel that I was to blame, and something must be wrong with me or men would not take advantage of me in that way. Though I viewed myself to blame, I developed a mistrust toward men. I did not despise men, but I would not totally commit myself emotionally to my boyfriends even though having sex with them was no problem.

Instead, I began to become emotionally attached to my girl-friends, and secretly I desired to be with them sexually because I felt totally safe with them. It was the grace of God that I never became sexually involved with my girlfriends.

At age 19, I joined the Air Force. I viewed this as a perfect opportunity to escape my abusive past and start afresh in another part of the country.

At age 22, I was raped and sodomized by my boyfriend in the middle of the night. This deepened my mistrust toward men. Emotionally, I had written men off and was ready to convert to a life of lesbianism.

I was drained emotionally. Outwardly, I was very attractive but viewed my physical attributes as a curse. I hated anyone telling me how pretty I was and tried very hard to cover my femininity with men's clothes. I did not want to be a woman; it brought too much pain. I decided to commit suicide at age 23. If I went through with my plans, however, I knew my soul would be lost for eternity. The only godly example in my life, the woman my mother had asked to care for me, told me that God was real. I cried out to God. Two weeks later a godly woman invited me to church. That day, I gave my life to Christ.

Outwardly, my life had been great. I had a military career; I was pursuing a college education in psychology; I was considered the life of the party; money was always in my pocket; I had a new car, a few good friends, and many associates. Inwardly, however, I was empty. When I received Christ, the void disappeared. I still had the same problems: not trusting men, feeling unwanted, and not appreciating myself as a woman.

Now 29 years old, I have been delivered from the rejection, which I received in the womb; the shame and guilt of the molestations; the molestations themselves; incest; the desire for homosexual relationships; the mistrust of men and prejudice. I have forgiven my father and the others.

I love my father with all my heart. I am so glad that I am a black woman, and I appreciate myself wholly for the first time in my life. I am still learning every day about who Christ made me to be.

I have come to know my purpose for living. I am now a licensed minister and youth minister who trains young people of different races and ages to discover their individuality through Christ without forsaking their natural heritage. I do this with no shame, and I am committed to sharing the goodness of the Lord Jesus.

As we can see from this woman's testimony, the roles of her parents and the instability of her home life tremendously impacted how she viewed herself. This opened her to the enemy's lies and his many snares. Through the influence of a godly woman, however, she came into a knowledge of the truth. She discovered the power of Jesus Christ to heal and restore.

African people have some very unique problems that affect our families in ways that you could understand only by being black in America. We are not looking for a pity party but perhaps an acceptance party as human beings created equal by God.

Why Black Men Feel Insignificant

Amos Wilson writes, "It is not class membership which plays the primary role in the mental development of the child but the parent-child, family-child relationship which does so."[6] Let's take a closer look at the family, especially the role of the father in relation to significance.

In her book, *Crisis in Masculinity,* Leanne Payne writes, "Whosoever does not accept himself (love himself aright) is necessarily turned inward upon himself. To be free to turn outward and love others, I must accept myself."[7] In order to destroy a family, race, or culture, one must attack the head who provides and protects that institution.

Black men have been so mentally abused that they hate themselves.

When society creates situations and circumstances for others to fail, society must be willing to take responsibility for what has been created. Amos Wilson feels very strongly about the connection between poverty and crime:

> The conditions under which African Americans live have been deliberately instituted by white America in order to accomplish definite ends.
>
> Poverty in the United States is a crime committed against the African-American population. White racism and other forms of discrimination against Africans are designed to maintain African Americans in relative and absolute poverty. Poverty represents the deliberate, vicious robbery, exploitation and extortion of the labor, wealth, and resources of the African community by European/White American community. Thus, if crime is "caused by poverty," the black criminality is crime which white criminality produced.[8]

Every man is responsible for his own behavior. My intention is not to excuse criminal behavior, but it is very important that we investigate the whole matter, giving everyone responsibility for the making of a criminal.

The wearing down of a man by making opportunities unequal and a normal family life extremely difficult will cause that man to feel inferior and insignificant.

When a man cannot find any significance for being and always experiences great difficulty just trying to survive, he will develop wrong beliefs as to what makes a person significant.

If society has convinced you that you are a person with no self worth, what can you possibly pass on to family members? The strong mental development that black families need so desperately must begin with freeing our men from mental enslavement.

Brothers, we must realize that our present conditions should not dictate our identity or our destiny. Our voices are needed at home to help others, especially our sons, to accept who they are. The women cannot do a job that calls for your God-given purpose. An old folk saying captures this important psychological insight: "A man is never a man until his father tells him he is a man."[9]

You Have a Purpose!

God knows who you are and why you are!

He has a purpose for your life on earth. Without Him you will never have the fulfillment you long for in your lifetime.

Life is too short to keep experimenting, hoping that one day you will mix the right ingredients. Why do we keep running from the only hope we have? My significance is not in my job, money, spouse, or children but in the One who created me with significance and personal worth.

Liberating yourself is a very simple decision. You must believe what God has said about you. Just as important, however, is *not* believing lies about yourself.

Scripture tells us what the Lord purposed even before we were born.

Praise be to the God and Father of our Lord Jesus Christ, who has blessed us in the heavenly realms with every spiritual blessing in Christ. For he chose us in him before the creation of the world to be holy and blameless in his sight. In love he predestined us to be adopted as his sons through Jesus Christ, in accordance with his pleasure and will – to the praise of his glorious grace, which he has freely given us in the One he loves (Ephesians 1:3-6, NIV).

The prophet Isaiah asked, "Who has believed our report?"

We need to submit ourselves to true brothers of the faith and allow the anointing of the Holy Spirit to break the yokes of bondage on our minds and make us free. The yoke is destroyed because of the anointing.

And it shall come to pass in that day, that his burden shall be taken away from off thy shoulder, and his yoke from off thy neck, and the yoke shall be destroyed because of the anointing (Isaiah 10:27).

Once our mental yokes have been broken, let's ask God to pour out His Holy Spirit upon us in an even greater measure. May God anoint us to "bind up the brokenhearted, to proclaim liberty to the captives, and the opening of the prison to them that are bound" (Isaiah 61:1).

In your search for truth, by all means get free – but don't stop there. Use what you have learned to release your brothers and sisters into the glorious freedom that awaits us in Christ.

Chapter Five

Winning the War for the Mind

A war is being waged against the minds of men to keep them mentally bound. These generational mindsets of satanic thinking must be destroyed.

Psychological warfare is used to influence or confuse the thinking, undermining the morale and unity of an enemy. Satan's strong tactical maneuvers attempt to keep the mentality of Africans – and Europeans – locked into one set pattern of thinking. This generational set pattern of thinking is called archetypes.

John and Paula Sanford, in *The Transformation of the Inner Man*, define archetypes and how they affect our behavior.

By an archetype we mean a ruling way of thinking, feeling, and acting, built by mankind into the common mentality we share; an archetype, therefore, being a device into the flesh of mankind, generally which acts upon us to control us individually.

Inside an individual, a habit or "practice" can be developed until it has an automatic, autonomous life. If, for example, the habit is jealousy, we may decide not to be jealous, only to find ourselves taken over and expressing jealousy anyway the next time we are caught off guard. That habit has obtained a life of its own in our flesh and does not want to die. It looms up and controls us whenever it is triggered, until and unless we break its hold. Some habits are so strong that fleshly willpower cannot break them; and so we discover anew our continuing need for the intervention of Jesus as our Lord and Savior.

An archetype is simply a habit or practice not inside an individual but in the flesh of mankind. An archetype (as we define it) is any developed way of thinking – a tradition, a cultural norm, an "empty philosophy," a habitual way of emoting and rationalizing – which can clamp upon individuals. Under the influence of an archetype, our minds become like preprogrammed computers, we develop tunnel vision, our wills are circumscribed, and our emotions are no longer those of our spirit or the Holy Spirit in us but they become outer-controlled, predictable, and usable.[1]

These programmed ways of thinking start out as a work of the flesh. After the flesh has been allowed to be active in that mindset, the powers of darkness can gain easy access to our minds and set up a stronghold.

Scripture tells us not to give place to the devil (Ephesians 4:27). The word place can also be interpreted as a window. When we leave the window of our soul (mind, will, and emotions) open and exposed to the enemy long enough, that enemy will take advantage of the opportunity to conquer our soul.

Our warfare is psychological (2 Corinthians 10:3-6) and spiritual.

> For we wrestle not against flesh and blood, but against principalities, against powers, against the rulers of the darkness of this world, against spiritual wickedness in high places (Ephesians 6:12).

In psychological warfare, the knowledge of the truth can make me free in some instances (John 8:32), depending on the depth of the stronghold. But when wicked spirits in high places begin to wrestle with our minds, we must wage war in the spirit with more powerful weapons or signal for reinforcements.

There are high places set up in the minds of Europeans who believe that they are superior to the world's majority population of non-whites. This set pattern and cultural norm has been so ingrained in their thinking process that the majority of the world's population (non-white) are viewed as the minority. This is just one of many archetypal thoughts that form the thinking of Euro-Americans. This sinful thinking has been passed down from generation to generation.

On the reverse side of this coin is the inferiority complex that plagues the non-white segments of society – that feeling and mindset of being a second class citizen and Christian.

As I mentioned, the black man has been mentally abused so long that he hates himself and the very race he was born into. These are sinful ways of thinking because whatever is not of faith is sin (Romans 14:23).

These are the thoughts the apostle Paul said we must cast down because they exalt themselves against the knowledge of God.

Getting Free

In order to be delivered from these set patterns, we must confess them as sin. If we call sin by any other name, we will seek other means and methods to eliminate it. By calling it sin, however, we can't get any remedy other than what's already been prescribed, the blood of Jesus Christ (1 John 1:7-9). What can wash away my sin? Nothing but the blood of Jesus!

What's my first step to eliminating this sin? I must confess and let someone who has a good relationship with Jesus take authority over these archetypal thoughts and break the yoke in Jesus' name. In confessing, it's vital that we dig deep and uproot the cause of the bondage to ensure that it's destroyed at the root. If we deal with it superficially, we will get only temporary relief.

If a demon is present because the window of our soul has been open to evil forces for a prolonged time, it must be cast out in the name of Jesus (Mark 16:17). Remember, once you successfully cast out an evil spirit, that's only a means to an end – not the end itself. Reprogramming the brain's computer with godly principles and truth will complete the deliverance of the mind (Romans 12:1,2).

The blood of Jesus washes and cleanses us of sin. The Bible also speaks of a washing of water by the Word to continually cleanse us after the blood washes us clean initially (Ephesians 5:26). As we bring healing to the internalized images and archetypes, both blacks and whites who really want to be free must remove any outer images that don't represent truth at every level.

We must bring proper balance and provide each other with an accurate account of historical and biblical truth. Black children need to have a proper image of their culture. Everyone in agreement with the truth must destroy these stereotypical images.

Parents and teachers should not wait until February and Black History Month to tell our children about their rich heritage as descendants of Africans. Our history and cultural practices far exceed the 200 years of American history that is ingrained in our children. The limited teaching they receive unconsciously causes our children to think we were born slaves and that was the way it was supposed to be.

Children begin to accept this inferior status without consciously making a decision to think this way. They are led to believe they were illiterate savages running around in Africa with no existing civilization. Parents, pastors, and teachers – remember that our non-white and white children need the truth to deliver their already uninformed minds.

Homosexuality

I am not going to spend time trying to convince anyone that homosexuality is a sin against one's own body and give scriptures to prove the point. People know when they are sinning but have simply chosen to exchange the truth for a lie. I want to speak to those who are struggling with this spirit, believe that it is sin, and want to be liberated from homosexuality in thought or act.

You can't be free from chains that you want to keep. If you believe you're okay the way you are, this section is not for you. If you have been secretly battling homosexual thoughts and acts, I want to minister some liberating solutions to end the battle.

Whenever people give up the fight for their freedom, they immediately try to convince everyone else that it's all right to yield to their flesh. The real problem, however, is you were not properly equipped to fight and guard your thought life. As a result, it became easier and less confusing to rationalize having an alternative lifestyle that Scripture does not sanction. Part of the problem begins in the first place of social adjustment, the home.

I saw a young man on a talk show who was in full drag as a homosexual. His mother, who did not have a husband, painted his fingernails and dressed him in girl's clothing at night for bed. Eventually, he gave in to his mother's influence. His mind told him, "This is what you should become because it feels more natural than who you really are." Families like this are very instrumental in creating an environment for the breeding of weak and overly effeminate qualities in boys.

Fathers Affirm Gender

Did you notice that no man was in the home of this black mother who had a son and daughter? There was no man for him to see standing while using the toilet, so he probably did what he saw and sat down like the females in the house. There was no masculine example for him to follow and to affirm his gender.

There are other reasons why boys grow up to become homosexual, but I am mainly concentrating on the role the father plays in the gender identity of his children. "As iron sharpens iron, so one man sharpens another" (Proverbs 27:17, NIV). Boys need the sharpening that only another man can provide.

God did not design women to do certain things. When God created us, He put in us everything needed to fulfill the purpose for which we were created. There are some things that no one else can do because they were not designed by the Manufacturer of Life to perform in that manner.

The male-man, as Dr. Myles Munroe refers to him, has the right equipment to bring proper gender identity to both male and female. Whenever the man is out of place and position, however, everyone else will be out of place and position.

Remember the testimony of the young woman in the previous chapter? Her father's incestuous relationship with her also brought about the gender confusion that she experienced. She felt comfortable and safe with women because her father did not do his God-given job in raising her.

Confusion sets in as to who you are because the man doesn't know who he is. If he knew who he was, he would not be mistreating and abusing what he should be affirming and loving. That's why women are protesting today for equal rights. Men have not allowed women to be what God intended – equal but different. When men take their place and position as men, everyone and everything else will also be in order.

Almost half of our African-American homes are headed by females. Our men are being set up to leave home in an effort to annihilate the black family. Dr. Jawanza Kunjufu comments in his work, *Countering the Conspiracy to Destroy Black Boys*, "I believe the motive for the conspiracy is white male supremacy, but as Alice Walker has commented, 'If you think the only reason for our problem is because of somebody else, you have given them a compliment they do not fully deserve.' You can blame white men for a portion of the problem, but white men do not determine if our boys wash dishes and clean up their rooms."[2]

While there are many conspiracies and plots working against the African in this world, we must not continue to allow the excuse of the white man's actions to displace us from our position in our families.

We need to recognize just how we have been set up and tricked right out of our homes when the boy grows up without his father. That boy needs to appropriately touch the man in his life where masculinity can be caught and transferred to him.

When that man is absent from his son, there is no one who can adequately sharpen him into manhood. I know we have some outstanding role models who were raised by mothers only. I'm simply pointing out the fact that it's not her job alone. Because she is doing it alone, we are creating problems in gender confusion among our children.

Distorted Roles

The man's responsibility starts when he's a child. If he is not a responsible man, it's because he was not taught responsibility as a child. Our young men grow up with the wrong attitudes and beliefs about household chores and responsibilities. Many young men today can't take care of themselves in many simple household responsibilities such as cooking, washing clothes and dishes, and keeping their room clean.

We have sent them the message that these roles are female responsibilities only – to engage in housework is feminine, not masculine. I was raised by my grandmother who taught me how to clean the entire house. She also taught me how to cook so when I went out on my own, I was able to do man things that most brothers rely on women to do for them.

Knowing how to perform these household responsibilities has enabled me to be a real blessing to my wife and children. My son is learning the importance of being responsible in the household by my example. You will not hear any complaints about my lack of masculinity from my wife because I am capable of sharing in household responsibilities.

Brothers, we have been instructed by the wrong teachers in our beliefs concerning being responsible at home. My father-in-law told me that his father said, "The only time a man should be caught in the kitchen is to eat." Many brothers have been told, by words and deeds, that the kitchen is the woman's place. The woman does have a place, positioned with the man to rule and dominate the earth together (Genesis 1:26). These distorted views of responsibilities have led women into the move to become liberated. When men are out of position, this puts our women in wrong roles and positions.

The sisters should know by the actions of the brothers that they're already liberated! Men, we must shoulder the responsibility that we're to blame for the Woman's Equal Rights Movement.

We expect our women to work outside the home to satisfy our lust for material gain and still come home and do *all* the duties of a wife and mother. This is part of the reason why we have such a conflict between men and women in this society.

Brothers, we need to unlearn the things we were taught by bad examples. God made the woman to be our helper, one suitable for us. Let's stop misusing our help. Remember, the woman is God's idea (Genesis 2:18).

◢ Lash Out

...Hicks, author of *The Masculine Journey*, contends, "...ct out some of the unconscious pain they have accumulated with violence."[3]

When a man is wounded and hurt, he responds like an animal that's been wounded and hurt. When you approach a wounded animal, it prepares to defend itself even though you may be trying to bring some comfort and help.

Many men strike out violently due to conscious and unconscious pain they have accumulated throughout the years.

But I don't believe there is a man in America who has experienced the wounds that the Africans have received since coming to these shores.

America rallies around the holocaust of the European Jews, but America doesn't show the same concern for the millions of Africans who died coming to America. The word holocaust means a great or total destruction of life. Millions of black people lost their lives through slavery. This is not just a holocaust but the greatest destruction of human life ever recorded in history.

Please don't misunderstand me. I am looking for neither pity nor sympathy from America. I do want to look at the woundedness of a much neglected people, however.

While speaking with a brother who hosts a television program here in Lancaster, I heard how he now watches his twenty year old go through the same things he had to go through when he was twenty. I believe my brother was speaking with concern and from a troubled and wounded soul.

This is the reason why we just can't get over it and move on. It would be like covering the wound from a 357 Magnum with only a band-aid; it won't do the job.

The powerlessness that black men experience in this country is a part of the wound they carry day after day.

When you deliberately keep a man from being what God put him here to be, you create problems for yourself. If I have to be treated as a sub-human, then that's how I'm going to act and respond. Black men are not committing violent acts of crime such as rape and murder because they enjoy this and want to show how powerful they are. What is really being expressed is the frustration of powerlessness.

The black man says, "I can't be the man I was put here to be," not because he doesn't know how but because the system has been set up for him to fail. That's why the jails are filled with predominately black men. The system has been set up for us to fail, starting in elementary school. (I recommend you read *Countering the Conspiracy to Destroy Black Boys* by Dr. Jawanza Kunjufu for more information.)

I believe African people suffer from a strong spirit of rejection. Many of us would probably say, "I don't need to be accepted by Euro-Americans." Even those who have found other means to cope probably still suffer from rejection. This spirit has been passed down throughout our generations. The previous chapter shared the testimony of a young woman who had the desire to be white because she saw the struggle and hardships of being black in America.

Everyone wants to be accepted for who he or she is. When this doesn't occur, rejection sets in. African people are not looking for a pity party but perhaps an acceptance party as men created equal by God.

We must break the power of rejection in our lives. By invoking the presence of Christ, we can bring healing to our wounded souls to enable us to accept who we are.

Exposure to the Truth

I recall hosting a sister from Africa in our home one evening. She began to show me photographs of her husband and children in Africa. As I looked at these photos, mental warfare began because of the media's distortion of Africa (or its one-sided, narrow perception) and all that I had been told and taught.

I saw houses like some here in America, along with scenes of her children in a park with green grass. She didn't have any idea what was going on in my head while she showed me these photos.

This is what we need – exposure to what really is and not what we have received from the distorted images shown to us by Euro-Americans through their loaded weapon, the media.

Allow your brain to be washed with the truth and come into the true knowledge of who you are.

Remember, the deep damage is not caused by the woundedness of our soul, *but our reactions to the wound*. This is tied into the way we think and feel. We must bring healing to the wound itself, but we must also war against the strongholds in our minds. If we heal the wounds, the black on black violence will stop. The self-hatred and inferiority complex within will be removed. Respect for self, God, and others will be restored.

Westernized mindsets and influences have short-circuited the moral values and the respectful cultural belief system that were followed by our forefathers in Africa.

As you read the following poem, listen to the author's frustration over old wounds and his battle with anger. His only hope is found in Christ.

A Cold World

It's a cold world in which I live.
Just learning to survive takes all I can give.
Can I stay strong in this jungle called earth?
Or will I lay down, forgetting the gift of my birth?

As I start to see as I've never seen before,
Out of life arises anger from a very old sore.
I want and ought to love, but anger has control,
Making me fight back, in a world – oh so cold!

Black and White – an issue that needs to be fixed.
My people suffer but don't realize that they're sick.
Victims of a brain washing,
the most massive ever performed.
Problems that never existed in Africa, our true home.

I cry out for justice, but my cry is never heard.
To be Black and proud is totally absurd.
I'm learning who I am, have been, and where I must go.
Lord, strengthen and enlighten me –
Your blessings please bestow.

In the struggle may I prosper, build up and not break down
My brothers and my sisters, may love in us abound.
We will be resurrected, through Christ's love and sacrifice-

A strong and proud Black people,
Who have weathered all life's tests.

Everett White

Through Christ we can weather every test, emerging from them stronger than ever before. Jesus Christ provides hope – and the power to break mental strongholds that have bound us for years. Don't get discouraged if you lose a battle. With Christ we are victors who are destined to win the war.

Chapter Six

You Are More Than
What You Have Become

The Lion King is a movie about a lion ruler, Mufasa, and his son Simba, a naive and curious cub who just can't wait to be king.

The opening scene shows two lions who are brothers. The noble Mufasa is contrasted with Scar, his jealous and rebellious sibling. Scar refused to be present at the birth of the future king, Simba. After the birth of this heir, Uncle Scar plotted to destroy the king and his son.

Uncle Scar easily deceived Simba to go to the forbidden darkness to see what he believed to be an elephant burial ground. This location turned out to be the place where the hyenas were banished. With these destroyers out of the land, Mufasa's kingdom flourished. His territory, known as the circle of life, continued unbroken.

Simba and a friend almost lost their lives on this dangerous journey. Their reckless antics also endangered the king, who came to rescue them from the threat of the hyenas.

Undaunted by failure on his first attempt to seize the throne, Scar promised the hyenas that they would not see another hungry day if they would endorse him as king and become a part of the conspiracy to kill Mufasa.

Simba, the king's son, was again deceived and set up by Uncle Scar, someone whom he naively trusted. Mufasa again came to his son's rescue, which is exactly what Scar had hoped for. He eagerly watched, anticipating that a stampede would kill both father and son.

Exhausted after rescuing his son and carrying him to safety, Mufasa needed help from Scar. Hanging from the side of a mountain, the king pleaded for his life. Instead of saving the king, Scar clawed his brother's hands and watched him fall to his death.

Simba hurried to his father only to find him dead. As the cub lay down beside the lifeless body, Uncle Scar appeared and blamed him for his father's death. Receiving this lie and fearing for his life, Simba didn't know what to do.

"Run away and never return," Scar told him, clearing the way for him to ascend to the throne as king.

Scar, who received the kingship by deception, lies, and murder, allowed the hyenas to live among the inhabitants of Pride Rock. The lions ate the animals, and the animals ate the vegetation, and life kept producing life, so everyone was content in this circle of life.

But the hyenas, along with King Scar, turned this circle of life into a circle of death. Soon they had destroyed all life in the kingdom. Meanwhile Simba escaped after orders were given to kill him.

Exhausted, Simba passed out in the middle of the desert. A warthog and meerkat befriended him. Forgetting his responsibilities to the kingdom he was born to rule, Simba adopted a carefree lifestyle. This new life also had its drawbacks, however. Simba, who once ate like a lion, adapted the less than palatable diet of his companions. As he grew into adulthood, Simba completely abandoned his destiny as king of the circle of life.

One day, while hunting for food, the lioness that Simba once played with as a cub saw one of Simba's new friends and began chasing him for her food. Simba rescued his friend and discovered that this lioness was his old playmate, Nala.

After they got reacquainted, she told him what his Uncle Scar had allowed to happen to Pride Rock. The hyenas had completely destroyed everything, turning the kingdom into a wasteland. Nala tried to convince Simba to return home and take his rightful place as king. Everyone thought Simba was dead. Simba, however, had grown accustomed to his new life. Because he feared his past failures, he refused to go back. She challenged him to think about who he really was and urged him to take his rightful place as king.

Simba went off, pondering what she had said to him.

Rafiki, a wise mystic baboon, discovered that Simba was still alive and went to help him reclaim his true destiny in the circle of life. The baboon began to taunt Simba because the lion did not know who he was. Afraid of the hurts of his past, he had chosen to become someone else.

Rafiki led Simba to a lake and helped him to see the reflection of his father. His father appeared to him in a vision and said, "Simba, you have forgotten me." Simba said, "I haven't forgotten you, Father." "You have forgotten who you are, so you have forgotten me," his father replied.

Reminding him of his destiny, Simba's father made this key statement: "You are more than what you have become." He urged his son, "Remember who you are!"

After Rafiki had knocked some sense into Simba by banging his head with a stick, he journeyed home to take his rightful position in the circle of life. Upon returning he learned that all Nala had told him about the destruction of Pride Rock was true. Lies, deception, and murder had turned the circle of life into a circle of death.

Simba had to face the past he ran from. His father's death wasn't really his fault, but he had believed Uncle Scar's lie. Knowing the truth, Simba decided to dethrone Uncle Scar and his subjects to assume his rightful position as the true king.

Overhearing Scar referring to them as the enemy, the hyenas turned on Scar and attacked him. Rafiki told Simba that it was time to take his position on the same mountain where his father and mother had summoned the kingdom to acknowledge his birth.

Simba walked into his destiny with a majestic roar over Pride Rock. The kingdom that he inherited was now barren and filled with death everywhere. As the king rose to his position, the lioness roared in agreement that he took back what was rightfully his. After the king took his throne, life was eventually restored. The circle of life that his father once ruled completely replaced the circle of death.

Remember Who You Are

Mufasa told his son, "You are more than what you have become!"

Because of lies, kidnapping, and slavery, Africans have become a people created out of a lying image that doesn't reflect the truth of who they really are.

Like Uncle Scar, Uncle Sam has caused us to run from who we really are. We have assumed the role he has projected onto us. Africans in America and in other parts of this world have been robbed of the knowledge of self, creating a poor self-image.

Dr. Stan DeKoven writes, "Self-image has to do with how a person thinks about himself/herself, about his intellectual ability, physical characteristics, personality, and talents."[1]

Dr. Frances Cress Welsing concurs on the importance of self-image: "The self-image is the core from which all else evolves in the brain-computer. Thus, the deep self-image is the key concern of the psychiatrist."[2]

How a people view themselves is the foundation for all other relationships.

Convincing black people that they are cursed by God and deserve to be treated like animals has greatly contributed to the forgetfulness of who we were before our forced captivity. Slave masters concealed the truth and caused division among our own families. We must go back to where we started and begin again. I'm not saying that we need to go back to Africa to live, but we must recapture the collective thinking as a people to reestablish our heritage and the economic stability once revered by Africans.

Simba asked Rafiki, "Who are you?" Rafiki answered, "The question is, who are you?" In other words, this heir to the throne didn't even know his identity – or his destiny.

Simba was told that his father wasn't dead, but he lived in him. "Look inside yourself," he was told. "You are more than what you have become."

Ancestral Traditions

African people for hundreds of years have been involved in ancestral worship. Even before the Europeans arrived in Africa, we had a belief in and a concept of God. The New Testament records that the gospel went into Ethiopia (Acts 8) before it entered Europe (Acts 10) via the house of Cornelius, a Roman.

Chief Musamaali-Nangoli exposes a commonly held lie among Europeans:

One of the most monstrous lies perpetuated about Africans by Europeans, is that they didn't know God! That until the missionaries arrived, the Africans lived the life of a pagan and the existence of God was unknown to him. This is a huge mountain of a lie! The Africans knew God. They wouldn't have had names for God if they didn't know him in the first place.[3]

I recommend that you read this man's book, *No More Lies About Africa*. He brings out the truth and the traditions of our people before our American experience and gives us a good foundation that must be reestablished among our people.

We must set the record straight concerning our relationship to God before our American experience. Much of our mental bondage has come as a result of lies and misconceptions about our motherland and our religious practices.

Those who are dead continue to live in us through the righteousness of God that they have imparted to us. "The memory of the just is blessed: but the name of the wicked shall rot" (Proverbs 10:7).

Those things that have been imparted by our ancestors can and will live on as memories, both good and bad.

What we must do is separate the ungodly traditions from the godly ones and make sure that our traditions can pass the test of Scripture. All truth comes from God and will be able to stand the scrutiny of the Word of God.

Learn from the Past

Simba was told that his father lived in him and he needed to look inside himself (to his past) and remember who he was. His father repeated, "Remember!" as his voice faded.

Simba told Rafiki that going back meant he must face his past. Rafiki wisely answered that one can run from his past or learn from it.

The apostle Paul told the Romans, "For everything that was written in the past was written to teach us, so that through endurance and the encouragement of the Scriptures we might have hope" (Romans 15:4, NIV). God also commanded His people to transfer knowledge to the next generation. He intended that this would continue throughout our history (Deuteronomy 6:6-9).

Why do you think God chose Abram? The Lord had this confidence in the patriarch: "For I know him, that he will command his children and his household after him, and they shall keep the way of the Lord, to do justice and judgment" (Genesis 18:19). Abram knew how to impart truth to the generation coming after him.

97

There has always been a conspiracy to keep black people from knowing who they really were before coming to America. If you can successfully conceal and destroy the past of a people, you can do great harm to their future.

If I don't know where I came from, how can I properly prepare for where I am going? If I don't know where I am going, how will I know when I get there? Selah! Because we lack knowledge of our destiny, historically and biblically, we grow frustrated with our hit and miss existence.

In the same way, the African people must look back before we can move ahead. Once we find out where we are on the map, then we can move ahead. When a man is lost, he must first establish his present location. After he knows where he is, then he can set out in the right direction.

Take Your Rightful Place

In order for African men and women to reach their destinations in life, they must stop where they are and look at the map of history to discover where they are now standing. Then they can proceed in the right direction.

Rafiki told the young lion Simba, "It is time!" Simba went back to challenge Uncle Scar and take his rightful position as king.

History proves that African men and women were rulers of dynasties – pharaohs, kings, and queens. It is time for the sons of the King to stop living among the warthogs and meerkats of the world. It is time for us to change our diets physically and spiritually and begin to eat what is fit for royalty.

When we did not know who we were, like Simba, we subsisted on what others gave us to eat. Now we must move past surviving to living as God intended.

As Simba returned home to challenge Uncle Scar for his rightful position, so you and I must challenge Uncle Sam for what's rightfully ours. Our ancestors gave their sweat and blood and died on American soil for the comforts of others.

It is time for us to come out of a world filled with greed, covetousness, and murderous hyenas. We are not to worship our departed ancestors, but we should take the righteous memories and apply them to our lives. When we forget our ancestors and what they sacrificed for us, we forget who we are. Remembering, however, puts us in a position today to bring a change to our world and to our people.

Remember who you are!

Look inside yourself. You are much more than what you have become!

Chapter Seven

Jesus, the Radical Revolutionary

During the 15 years I have been a part of the Church of Jesus Christ, I have heard many comments about the weakness of this institution, especially among the male members.

During the captivity of Africans in America, the majority of the Church proved to be what she has been accused of – weak.

Scripture speaks emphatically that we are to love and esteem our brother higher than ourselves (Philippians 2:3,4). Yet, during slavery, so-called Christians would not speak up and voice the Word of God concerning the mistreatment and cruel punishment of His people. (There were some rare exceptions, such as Charles Finney.)

In fact, Maryland's Act of 1671 stated that a black's religious conversion did not change the status of a slave. The audacity of man to discriminate and manipulate the grace of God for his own benefit reinforces the fact that satanic influences orchestrated the Euro-American slave institution. Even the power of God cannot change a man's will; this must be of his own volition. The implementation of this law reveals that their hearts were convicted and challenged to change but they chose to harden their hearts, and the bondage continued.

Christians misused and misquoted the Word of God in an effort to convince blacks that they were a people cursed with dark skin. In fact, Scripture points out something entirely different. Let's look at Elisha's servant who became greedy and was cursed with leprosy.

Gehazi, the servant of Elisha the man of God, said to himself, "My master was too easy on Naaman, the Aramean, by not accepting from him what he brought. As surely as the Lord lives, I will run after him and get something from him."

So Gehazi hurried after Naaman. When Naaman saw him running toward him, he got down from the chariot to meet him. "Is everything all right?" he asked.

"Everything is all right," Gehazi answered. "My master sent me to say, 'Two young men from the company of the prophets have just come to me from the hill country of Ephraim. Please give them a talent of silver and two sets of clothing.'"

"By all means, take two talents," said Naaman. He urged Gehazi to accept them, and then tied up the two talents of silver in two bags, with two sets of clothing. He gave them to two of his servants, and they carried them ahead of Gehazi.

When Gehazi came to the hill, he took the things from the servants and put them away in the house. He sent the men away and they left. Then he went in and stood before his master Elisha.

"Where have you been, Gehazi?" Elisha asked.

"Your servant didn't go anywhere," Gehazi answered.

But Elisha said to him, "Was not my spirit with you when the man got down from his chariot to meet you? Is this the time to take money, or to accept clothes, olive groves, vineyards, flocks, herds, or menservants and maidservants? Naaman's leprosy will cling to you and to your descendants forever." Then Gehazi went from Elisha's presence and he was leprous, as white as snow (2 Kings 5:20-27, NIV).

Gehazi and his descendants would be cursed with leprosy, as white as snow, forever! This diffuses the argument about being cursed with black skin.

The Toughest Thing on Earth

The reputation of the Church must change because Jesus Christ is not weak! The Church is the most powerful organism on planet earth today.

Jesus said, "I will build my church; and the gates of hell shall not prevail against it" (Matthew 16:18).

The phrase "the gates of hell," a common idiom in the Greek world, was used to convey the idea of the strongest possible force.

To people who were familiar with the idiom, the effect of associating it with Jesus' small band of disciples must have been quite startling. It was as if Jesus had said, "Until now you have known nothing mightier than the gates of hell, but I am about to create a new thing – My Church – against which the gates of hell will be impotent."

What does this mean to us? Author Barry Chant says, "The church is the toughest thing on earth."[1] Well then, what has happened to this mighty force against which the gates of hell would not be able to prevail?

The Church has lost its focus on the Founder of the Church.

Pictures of Jesus don't portray the Son of God as a man's man. He's looked upon as a weak sissy who allows anybody to mistreat Him. All He would do is turn the other cheek.

Dr. Jawanza Kunjufu researched the reason why most black men don't go to church and compiled his work in the book, *Adam! Where Are You?* Dr. Kunjufu had an overnight retreat with some brothers and 21 reasons were extrapolated and discussed. Let's examine one reason why most black men don't go to church – homosexuality.

> Several of the brothers said that the church is made of women, elders, children, and sissies. You notice most of the brothers that play the organ or piano or sing in the choir, how they got their butt going up in the air. They love waving their open hand. No wonder they believe in turning the other cheek; they probably want to be kissed on it. They can't defend themselves.[2]

This is why we must look closely at Jesus Christ and get a proper view of the institution He founded.

Jesus was a radical revolutionary. Let's look at the definitions of radical and revolutionary. According to *Webster's New World Dictionary*, radical means "of or from the root or roots; going to the foundation or source of something." Revolutionary means "the bringing out or constituting a great or radical change."

In light of these definitions, Scripture shows Jesus to be a man who went to the source of the problem. (See my book,

The Roots of Deliverance.) Jesus opposed the worldly views and hypocritical religious leaders of His day.

He believed in keeping the laws of the land. When challenged about paying taxes, He said, "Render therefore unto Caesar the things which are Caesar's; and unto God the things that are God's" (Matthew 22:21). Jesus kept the law by paying tribute to the ruler of the land. He knew how to respect those in authority.

Righteous Anger

When the Jews disrespected and broke the laws that pertained to the kingdom of His Father, however, Jesus showed another side to His character.

> And the Jews' passover was at hand, and Jesus went up to Jerusalem, and found in the temple those that sold oxen and sheep and doves, and the changers of money sitting: And when he had made a scourge of small cords, he drove them all out of the temple, and the sheep, and the oxen; and poured out the changers' money, and overthrew the tables; And said unto them that sold doves, Take these things hence; make not my Father's house an house of merchandise. And his disciples remembered that it was written, The zeal of thine house hath eaten me up (John 2:13-17).

Jesus found men in the temple, His Father's house, making money off those who came from all over the country to sacrifice and worship the Father. They were exchanging currency from one country to another in order to buy what was necessary in Jerusalem.

Instead of this being a time of worship and consecration to God, men were capitalizing on the needs the worshipers had upon arriving from many different places.

Angered at what was going on, Jesus made a whip out of cords and confronted the problem. I don't think Jesus pleaded with the moneychangers, "Please leave My Father's house." He didn't give a weak speech or to try to negotiate with them. Instead, He drove out those who were defiling the temple of God. A weak, sissified man would not overturn tables like He did. Jesus went into the temple alone. We read nothing about Jesus having a gang with Him like young men do today.

Scripture admonishes us to be angry, but don't sin (Ephesians 4:26). It is not a sin to be angry. The way we allow anger to affect us, however, determines if we are in sin.

When black people begin to view their history and discover the deceptions and conspiracies against them, they have every right to be angry. That anger should not cause anyone to sin against the kingdom of God, however.

We must be careful that we don't become like those who have oppressed us.

I read somewhere that black people would comment, "They did it to us, so we do it to them." We must remember that they are not our teachers; God is! When you hate and become racist, you are being taught by the wrong teacher and you need to be educated because you are now acting like an animal.

Telling It Like It Is

When Jesus spoke to the religious leaders of His day, this Man did not have any problems calling it like He saw it. Jesus told the crowds and His disciples about the teachers of the law who didn't practice what they preach.

Jesus said, "The greatest among you will be your servant. For whoever exalts himself will be humbled, and whoever humbles himself will be exalted" (Matthew 23:11,12).

Not much has changed today with our spiritual leaders. Many ministers are being served instead of serving the people. They want to serve the Word of God only and then let everybody else wait on them, hand and foot.

Jesus, who is our example, served the people naturally and spiritually.

To be exalted in the kingdom of God, Jesus said we must humble ourselves or aim for the seat of the servant. The best way to be brought down to nothing is to exalt yourself or aim for the exalted seat of prestige.

Jesus called the teachers of the law many things to describe their hypocrisy.

Woe to you, teachers of the law and Pharisees, you hypocrites! You clean the outside of the cup and dish, but inside they are full of greed and self-indulgence.

Blind Pharisee! First clean the inside of the cup and dish, and then the outside also will be clean.

Woe to you, teachers of the law and Pharisees, you hypocrites! You are like whitewashed tombs, which look beautiful on the outside but on the inside are full of dead men's bones and everything unclean.

In the same way, on the outside you appear to people as righteous but on the inside you are full of hypocrisy and wickedness (Matthew 23:25-28, NIV).

Notice that Jesus' focus went beyond what the people could see outwardly. He addressed the issues of the heart.

Jesus the Radical struck at the roots.

The religious leaders in Jesus day were no different than our own. They may look good outwardly, but on the inside they are full of greed and self-indulgence. Jesus said you could also find in them everything unclean! Looking at the Church today, it's not difficult to see that the leaders are full of something other than the righteousness of God. The people will have the spirit of their leaders.

Read Matthew 23 in its entirety. You will discover that Jesus Christ was not a weak Man who was afraid to speak out against the hypocrisy of His day.

Most of our so-called "leaders" in the church are afraid to rock the boat.

I heard a father in the faith say, "Not only will I rock the boat, I will sink it!" Many of the church leaders are scared. In the name of something other than fear, however, they excuse themselves for not confronting the issues that plague us as a people. The revolutionary brings a radical change to whatever needs to be altered.

Jesus Christ is the most radical revolutionary to bring to the world system. This Man was willing to stand alone if necessary. He knew that no one could take His life before His time. When it was time for Him to die, He would lay down His own life, and He had power to take His life again (John 10:17,18).

Born to Rule

Jesus' own people turned Him over to Pilate to be crucified.

Jesus said, "My kingdom is not of this world. If it were, my servants would fight to prevent my arrest by the Jews. But now my kingdom is from another place."

"You are a king, then!" said Pilate. Jesus answered, "You are right in saying I am a king. In fact, for this reason I was born, and for this I came into the world, to testify to the truth. Everyone on the side of truth listens to me."

"What is truth?" Pilate asked. With this he went out again to the Jews and said, "I find no basis for a charge against him" (John 18:36-38, NIV).

Jesus spoke of another kingdom, which led Pilate to remark, "You are a king, then!"

Jesus' answer is awesome. We can really begin to understand the purpose of the Church in the earth today as we examine their conversation. First, Jesus proclaimed that He was a king. As a matter of fact, He said that He was born to be a king! If a man is born to be a king, this means that he has a kingdom or domain over which to rule.

Genesis 1:26 confirms the fact that God created the African in the Garden of Eden to have dominion, along with his woman, over the earth. We were born to rule over those things designated by God in Scripture, not each other!

Na'im Akbar, in *Visions for Black Men*, writes, "You are prepared to lead a big community when you learn to lead a little community. You must first be a king in your personal kingdom. If you can't rule the kingdom on your feet, you can't lead a bigger kingdom."[3]

Notice that Jesus ruled the kingdom on His feet well. We must be in control of self before ruling anything else. One of the fruits of the Holy Spirit is self-control. I must be in control sexually and monetarily to qualify as king, according to God's standard (Deuteronomy 17:17).

Jesus said He was born, like us, to be king and to testify of the truth in the world. People on the side of truth can hear truth! You can only hear what you are in position to hear. We must position ourselves for the truth no matter what the cost.

Walk in Truth

Men are obligated to walk in and testify of the truth. Truth clears the way for liberation, it makes a path for harmony and love to prevail, and it builds a foundation for those who hear and embrace it.

Jesus was the manifestation of truth, or truth personified. You and I are to be truth personified and stand for nothing less than the truth.

There are no consistencies in lies; they offer nothing stable to build on.

Scientists can discover natural laws such as gravity because of the consistency of truth. Once a person starts walking in all known truth, his or her walk will have no room for inconsistencies.

That's why lies concerning our history as Africans are being exposed. The inconsistency of those lies can't continue to hold together under the power of truth. The truth will always outlive a lie! Pilate asked a question that many are asking today: "What is truth?"

Truth suggest conformity with facts or with reality. Reality is God, which is a fact. In order for men to know what truth is, they must first be willing to respond properly to truth. Pilate knew the truth that Jesus was innocent, but he allowed the people to choose a lie over the truth.

Pilate released the liar, Barabbas, and flogged the truth, Jesus.

Notice when lies are allowed to prevail, the truth is beaten down, held down, and suppressed. Isaiah's prophecy came to pass:

And judgment is turned away backward, and justice standeth afar off: for truth is fallen in the street, and equity cannot enter.

Yea, truth faileth; and he that departeth from evil maketh himself a prey: and the Lord saw it, and it displeased him that there was no judgment (Isaiah 59:14,15).

There is no justice in this world without God. Righteousness, or doing what is right, stands at a distance from those who need it.

Truth has fallen in the street to be trampled by those who love lies and live in darkness. The Word of God says, "Men loved darkness . . . because their deeds were evil" (John 3:19).

The liars who have embraced evil will not come to the light. In fact, they hate the light for exposing what they really are.

Whoever loves the truth and comes to the light shows everyone that his or her deeds had been done through God.

We must become a people who will be radical enough to present truth and nothing but the truth, so help us God!

We are under mandate by God, history, and our ancestors to tell the whole truth. We have an obligation to the generations coming after us to pass on the truth about who they really are. We can't suppress the truth for fear of what might happen to us for presenting it.

Under the mandate of truth every black leader – especially in the Church – has the obligation to tell the people they pastor who they are both scripturally and historically. We must stop being afraid and disliking who we are by saying this teaching is not necessary. We can't feel more obligated to our Euro-American friends than to our own people, culture, and Jesus Christ, the manifestation of Truth. Our purpose should be to walk in the truth at all times. Remember that the only people who will fight the truth are those who refuse to release the lie they have grown comfortable with.

If the truth will make you free, the lie will keep you in bondage.

Chapter Eight

Conquering Fear and Shame

Fear was first introduced in the life of man in the Garden of Eden. After the fall of man, the Lord God called to Adam and said, "Where are you?" Adam replied, "I was afraid because I was naked; so I hid" (Genesis 3:9,10, NIV). Adam now feared the voice he once communed with daily.

Sin, or disobedience to God's Word, brought fear on the scene and caused Adam to respond to God's voice in a totally different way than he had done before.

God's voice calls today and asks those of African heritage the same question: "Where are you? Why are you hiding from your responsibility to God and your people? Why do you overlook the bondages and mental enslavement of the people you say that you love?"

Disobedience and fear caused Adam's view of himself to change. Seeing his nakedness and experiencing fear for the first time, he hid from the One he once walked with in the cool of the day. The African/Edenic man Adam was once naked and not ashamed (Genesis 2:25). Author F. Earle Fox explains this:

> The shame associated with nakedness implies a vulnerability and impotence which strikes deeply into the human psyche. To have two persons who could be naked before each other and not feel that vulnerability is surprising indeed. It implies two persons, a man and a woman, who were secure of identity, purpose and worth.

> The nakedness of Adam and Eve is the openness of soul required by faith, openness to the truth.[1]

We must get back to the place of not being ashamed of who we are. We must not allow fear to keep us from being open to truth and speaking the truth. Being secure in our identity, purpose, and worth enables us to stay free of the binding effects of fear. The only way to be naked and not ashamed is to be obedient to God and commune with Him on a regular basis and to receive His strength in your weakness.

"God hath not given us a spirit of fear; but of power, and of love, and of a sound mind" (2 Timothy 1:7).

Brainwashing and fear have kept black ministers from speaking the whole truth to their congregations and others around them. Black pastors know more about Hebrews and Greeks than Africans and Egyptians. Yes, our spiritual heritage is relevant to who we are as a people, but that is only a part of our story.

God has given us leaders a spirit of power that we must use to empower our people. We must stop being dependent on those who have oppressed us. Leaders must stop living off the misery and hopelessness of our people while promising them something that they are incapable of producing. What we are capable of producing is the *whole truth,* which will begin to liberate oppressed people everywhere.

Don't you think that the people of God need to know that Moses didn't look like Charlton Heston? It is important that the people of God know who they are and what roles they represent in Scripture.

Is this emphasis on our heritage a source of enmity toward those of other races? Amos Wilson, in his book, *The Developmental Psychology of the Black Child, writes:*

> To be pro-black is not to be anti-white. To love oneself does not mean to hate others. It must be understood clearly that the genuine love of one's own ethnic group is the basis for the love of oneself, for the love of others and the basis for a loving personality in general.[2]

The fear of repercussive actions to the truth has so bound us that we don't say what needs to be said. Moreover, we get angry and betray those who will say it. Many will read this book and allow the brainwashing of their enslaved minds to speak against the truth. When we attack our brothers who speak truth, we are not attacking them but the truth that comes from God who is all Truth.

The Fear of Death

Any fear, but especially the fear of death, will keep us from going where God is trying to take us.

> Since the children have flesh and blood, he too shared in their humanity so that by his death he might destroy him who holds the power of death – that is, the devil – and free those who all their lives were held in slavery by their fear of death (Hebrews 2:14,15, NIV).

This fear of death caused African mothers to be overly protective of their sons during their captivity. The fear of lynching during that time has caused our mothers today to still operate out of a spirit of fear concerning their sons. Black mothers still fear the death of their children, hostile treatment by law enforcement, and imprisonment for undetermined sentences.

Once I was arrested after squabbling with police. As they tied me up and carried me to the squad car, my grandmother said, "Don't you hurt my boy." Our neighborhood knew what kind of treatment you could expect at the hands of police officers, and my grandmother made that known in her statement. A videotape captured Rodney King's beating, but thousands – perhaps millions over the decades – were not so fortunate to have a video with such astounding evidence.

The fear of death keeps men from being all they were purposed to be. This fear of dying keeps you from saying what needs to be said and doing what needs to be done. Dr. Myles Munroe speaks about God's intended purpose for death:

> Through sin, death began to do something that it was not supposed to do. It began to stop man's life. What God intended to be a blessing became a curse through man's disobedience. Sin made death go in reverse. Instead of ministering dying, it is causing killing.
>
> Killing is death before the completion of purpose. Dying is death after purpose has been fulfilled.
>
> The enemy (Satan) uses death for termination. God intended death for transition. The vast difference between the two is the result of death's change in position from servant to ruler. Death has become a threat because it is out of position.[3]

Death is out of position because of sin, and people now fear something that was designed to serve them. As Dr. Myles Munroe stated, the servant has become the ruler. The ruler (death) causes many to eat properly and exercise daily. While this is the right thing to do, have you considered the motive? Many people want to live a long time doing what they want – not living to fulfill God's purpose for their lives.

> Many are the plans in a man's heart, but it is the Lord's purpose that prevails (Proverbs 19:21, NIV).

We can plan to avoid premature death and to live a long time. If we are not doing the right thing God intended for our lives, however, death can kill us for being out of position.

When we allow fear to keep us out of the right position, we will meet the sting of death instead of peace in dying. Death becomes an ally when my position in God is right. In death I simply make the transition from one place to another.

Another reason Christians fear death is because they are not sure about their salvation. They are not sure what's really on the other side of death. Yes, we teach and preach about streets of gold, but no one wants to die in order to walk on them.

That's why at the first sign of any ailment, we run to the doctor for help instead of running to the Lord (2 Chronicles 16:12,13).

Fear looks for the worst to happen, and the torment of fear is the anticipation of what might happen. When you are truly following the Lord and in the right position, death has no power over you because Jesus Christ destroyed Satan who held the power of death. We are no longer slaves to the fear of death. We must stay in pursuit of our purpose and let death wait on us until we are finished with our God-given tasks (John 19:30).

The apostle Paul wrote to Timothy:

> For I am already being poured out like a drink offering, and the time has come for my departure. I have fought the good fight, I have finished the race, I have kept the faith.
>
> Now there is in store for me the crown of righteousness, which the Lord, the righteous Judge, will award to me on that day – and not only to me, but also to all who have longed for his appearing (2 Timothy 4:6-8, NIV).

We cannot finish the race if fear keeps us from ever leaving the starting block. Once we've begun the race, fear is just one of the many obstacles we will face on our way to the finish line. With a tenacious faith in God, however, we will overcome and receive the prize that awaits us.

Taking Responsibility

When we sin, we often allow the accompanying guilt and shame to paralyze us. Or, like Adam, we run from God – and our personal responsibility. In Jesus Christ, however, we have forgiveness of sins and the hope of restoration. Where race has divided us, we can turn to the One who "made the two one" and "destroyed the barrier, the dividing wall of hostility" (Ephesians 2:14, NIV). Reconciliation is possible, if we will work toward it.

Everyone needs to be responsible for his or her role in the world, government, society, community, and family. We can't continue to project the blame for our failures on others. We must focus on our individual responsibility for the messed up state of mankind and search our hearts to find what God has put inside of us to bring restoration.

Shifting blame onto others is as old as mankind itself. After the fall, God questioned the first couple about their sin.

> The man said, "The woman you put here with me – she gave me some fruit from the tree, and I ate it." Then the Lord God said to the woman, "What is this you have done?" The woman said, "The serpent deceived me, and I ate" (Genesis 3:12,13, NIV).

I like how God handled Adam's projection of blame onto his wife. After he blamed her, she projected the blame onto the serpent. But God brought them back to their personal responsibilities for the sin that had been committed.

Eve was responsible for listening to the serpent and for taking the forbidden fruit. Adam was responsible for taking what was forbidden from his wife and partaking of it. Read this passage again and see how God brought everyone involved back to personal responsibility for his or her actions (Genesis 3:11-19).

Euro-Americans owe the Africans an apology with restitution for their labor and the death of millions of their ancestors.

Africans must be willing to accept the apology and repentance of the Euro-Americans in order to bring godly reconciliation of the races. They must also have a forgiving heart for past – and present – injustices that have been suffered. Dr. Stan DeKoven includes this thought in his writing:

> However, if someone who has wronged you is unwilling to admit and repent, forgiveness that leads to reconciliation is not possible – or wise. How can you trust if there is no repentance? Reality is knowing that there is no guarantee of living "happily ever after" and humility is understanding that no one deserves forgiveness, including us![4]

The trust that the Africans had in the Europeans who came to Africa cannot and must not be reestablished until true repentance has been worked in their hearts by God. You can't trust a man who won't say, "Forgive me for the wrong that I have done." As Dr. Stan DeKoven said, to do so would not be wise.

The Bible states, "For it is time for judgment to begin with the family of God" (1 Peter 4:17, NIV). Reconciliation must begin with the church. Before the world can be ministered to, the church must first receive the ministry of reconciliation and restoration. This can only happen as everyone in the church begins to embrace the truth and stop covering sin with lies and fig leaves.

All of us are in need of forgiveness. Those who have mistreated others because of their race. Those who are angry or resentful at those who have oppressed minorities. Those who have known something needed to be done but stood by without acting.

Let us repeat David's prayer:

Have mercy upon me, O God, according to thy lovingkindness: according unto the multitude of thy tender mercies blot out my transgressions. Wash me thoroughly from mine iniquity, and cleanse me from my sin.

For I acknowledge my transgressions: and my sin is ever before me. Against thee, thee only, have I sinned, and done this evil in thy sight: that thou mightest be justified when thou speakest, and be clear when thou judgest.

Behold, I was shapen in iniquity; and in sin did my mother conceive me. Behold, thou desirest truth in the inward parts: and in the hidden part thou shalt make me to know wisdom.

Purge me with hyssop, and I shall be clean: wash me, and I shall be whiter than snow. Make me to hear joy and gladness; that the bones which thou has broken may rejoice. Hide thy face from my sins, and blot out all mine iniquities.

Create in me a clean heart, O God; and renew a right spirit within me. Cast me not away from thy presence; and take not thy holy spirit from me. Restore unto me the joy of thy salvation; and uphold me with thy free spirit. Then will I teach transgressors thy ways; and sinners shall be converted unto thee.

Deliver me from bloodguiltiness, O God, thou God of my salvation: and my tongue shall sing aloud of thy righteousness. O Lord, open thou my lips: and my mouth shall shew forth thy praise.

For thou desirest not sacrifice; else would I give it: thou delightest not in burnt offering. The sacrifices of God are a broken spirit: a broken and a contrite heart, O God, thou wilt not despise.

Do good in thy good pleasure unto Zion: build thou the walls of Jerusalem. Then shalt thou be pleased with the sacrifices of righteousness, with burnt offering and whole burnt offering: then shall they offer bullocks upon thine altar (Psalm 51:1-19).

Repent. Forgive. God will restore!

Black? White? Red? Yellow? Brown?

In order for reconciliation to be effective, we must begin to look beyond the color of a man's skin.

Allow the following poem to challenge your thinking.

Black? White? Red? Yellow? Brown?

Do you believe it's the color that makes a man?
Or do you judge him by the things he may do?
Or does his color mean that much to you?

Do you judge him by the stand he may make?
Or is your heart filled with too much bigotry and hate?

And why should you hate the color of a man?
Just because you don't know him or understand.

Every man is made the same,
No matter what may be his race or name.
Every man bleeds red blood just like you,
Even if he is colored blue.

Every man has dreams like you,
Even if you don't believe this is true.

And every man seeks the same,
To be treated with dignity and called by name.

Every man has thoughts like you,
No matter what color or how they look to you,

They call you Nigger, White devil, or Jew,
But this is not really all it is to you.

Men can't help being what color they are,
No more than a star could help being a star.

And if you could rid yourself of your bigotry and hate,
Who knows, you still may not be too late.

– Braxton Berkley

Chapter Nine

What Are You Producing?

God created the world with great diversity in plants, animals, and people. One thing they all had in common, however, was the ability to produce after their own kind.

Then God said, "Let the land produce vegetation: seed-bearing plants and trees on the land that bear fruit with seed in it, according to their various kinds." And it was so.

The land produced vegetation: plants bearing seed according to their kinds and trees bearing fruit with seed in it according to their kinds. And God saw that it was good....

So God created the great creatures of the sea and every living and moving thing with which the water teems, according to their kinds, and every winged bird according to its kind. And God saw that it was good....

And God said, "Let the land produce living creatures according to their kinds: livestock, creatures that move along the ground, and wild animals, each according to its kind." And it was so (Genesis 1:11,12,21,24,25, NIV).

God gave every living thing the ability to produce after its own kind. Apple seeds cannot produce oranges, and birds cannot produce cattle. But when He created you and me, God made us after His image and identified us with Himself. God's original purpose for you and me as human beings is to produce seed after our own kind, which is in the image of God.

A Downward Spiral of Sin

Dr. Stan DeKoven writes about the consequences of the fall and how it affected our ability to bear the image of God.

As humans we no longer carry the pure identity that Adam (mankind, including Adam and Eve) carried before the fall.

Sin in our seed, from Adam to now, has marred the image of God in us. Due to sin, we are all vulnerable to the damage, pain, and suffering from our forefathers.

In truth, we are a result of the "seed" that has been planted within us, both destructive through sin and productive through Christ.[1]

What we see in the world today is the result of seed reproducing after its own kind. We are witnessing a reproductive cycle of evil. That's why the brother I spoke with said he was seeing his twenty year old go through what he went through when he was twenty.

The apostle Paul told us that evil men and those who would seduce us into sin shall go "from bad to worse" (2 Timothy 3:13, NIV). A quick glance at the headlines of any newspaper tells us how much worse things have gotten.

Our families are suppose to be reproducing human beings after the image and likeness of God. But each passing year reveals a greater reproduction of evil in the hearts of men. Sometimes it seems that the human race acts more like animals than those who bear the image of God.

Parents, what are you raising, a potential leader who will one day help to solve many problems or a beast who will add to the problems that already exist? Our society places very little value on life. People are more concerned about money and things than the most precious creation of all, man. Invest in your children and place a vision in them to change the world.

Turning Our Backs on the Truth

People ask, "If God is really God, why does He permit this madness to exist?" We chose to neglect and turn our backs on the truth. Many years ago mankind chose to ignore God and what He said we must do to live an abundant life. Many have chosen to follow Frank Sinatra and "do it their way" instead of God's way.

Many believers today can't figure out why their lives are filled with confusion and in constant turmoil. Why do we lack the blessing of God? We are not doing exactly what the Word of God commands us to do.

The problem is we are not living right. We may be living well, but we're not living right. Our "good life" is slowly coming to an end because God cares more about our living right than living well. We can have both if we would only seek first the kingdom of God and His righteousness (Matthew 6:33).

Many in and out of the church have chosen to seek after things and add God later! We have been lied to and misinformed as to God's expectations for our lives. He wants to be the focus of our existence. Second place won't do.

If we want to turn our lives around, we must do it out of necessity. Stop making excuses for not doing the Word of God. Notice that I did not say reading the Word, which is absolutely necessary; *doing* what you read, however, will bring about the change you desire.

How satisfied are you with your life? If there's room for improvement, ask yourself, "Have I been reading and obeying the Word of God? Is the Lord pleased with my life?" If you're reading this book, that fact alone indicates hope for change. Stop being disobedient. Let's start reproducing what God intended for us to produce – a reflection of the image and identity of God.

I believe with the anointing and a willingness to obey the truth, there is hope for mankind, especially the Church.

Seeds of Health

In our ministry we believe in ministering to the total person: spirit, soul, and body.

Recently I concluded a series of studies on health and the nutritional needs of the human body. When we look at the sickness of society and the high cost of health insurance, it's not difficult to figure out that we are also reproducing seeds of bad health.

When each generation passes on wrong eating habits, it reproduces the same sickness and disease from past generations. I know that some of this is caused genetically, but we are what we eat as well.

I invited one of my children's male school teachers to assist me in a series of health studies. He shared, "Life begets life and death begets death." If you put life in, you will produce life. If you put death in, you will produce death. The foods in this country are made and raised to produce death in the human body.

Laboratory food additives and food processed in these labs may taste good, but our bodies were not designed for drugs and chemicals. For instance, the nitrates in processed meats such as bologna, salami, and hot dogs lead to disease and sickness of the body.

Amos Wilson, in *The Developmental Psychology of the Black Child*, writes, "It is possible that elements of the typical American diet may work against the mental and physical development of black children."[2]

Think about this. After you become sick, why does the doctor put you on a low sodium diet with fruits, vegetables, and distilled water? Why do we have to get sick before we eat properly? What we do after we're sick should be done as a way of life!

We are not told about natural ways to health and healing because the American Medical Association and pharmacists seek monetary gain. Many institutions are not concerned about you regaining your health.

If we were taught to put the right foods into our bodies, people would live in health and there would be little need for doctors and synthetic medicines given through pharmaceutical sales.

Milk Does a Body Good?

Milk commercials promote a dairy product that people can't properly digest. Drinking milk when you can't handle it may even cause negative psychological effects. Amos Wilson reported on the detrimental effects of milk on black children:

> Ingestion of milk by lactose intolerant children may cause irritability and confusion. A study done by the Johns Hopkins Medical School in 1971 indicated that 58 percent of the black children tested were unable to digest milk properly. Only 16 percent of the white children tested showed a similar inability to digest milk.
>
> The source of the trouble is a complex sugar found in milk, called lactose. In order to break down this sugar in the digestive tract, the body must produce an enzyme, lactase. While babies, regardless of race, do make lactase, most blacks will stop lactase production at about age two.
>
> Without lactase, this sugar simply passes down the intestine without being absorbed, and actually ferments right in the body, producing noxious chemicals . . .[3]

You would never know how terrible milk is for the human body by the misleading slogan, "Milk does a body good." Ingested milk causes mucus to build up in our bodies, which is one of the causes of constantly runny noses in our children. If your child can't seem to get rid of cold symptoms, you should stop his intake of milk and all dairy products. You might be surprised how quickly you notice the difference.

Someone who ministers with us recently visited an Oriental medicine doctor who also specializes in herbs. This person discovered that she was full of parasites because of drinking milk. Medical doctors are not trained to treat you for the root cause of illness. After your illness is detected by the doctor, it's often too far advanced to correct. You must become responsible for your own health and the health of your children.

The only good milk does for a body is when an infant drinks milk from his or her mother's breast. God gave women the ability to nourish their young. Ironically, humans are the only species that drink milk after being weaned and then drink another animal's milk.

Some of this information may challenge your thinking because of information you've already received, but let the psychological warfare begin and let truth emerge as the victor!

When you ingest dairy products, they go right through you because you are not biologically equipped to handle them after the age of two. Don't take the medicine that the pharmacist gives you in order to tolerate something you are intolerant of naturally. Leave that poison alone.

You can get all the calcium you need, which isn't that much, by eating fresh (organic if possible) fruit and uncooked vegetables, preferably juiced, and natural herbal supplements.

Eat Fresh Vegetables

We need to stay away from cooked foods as much as possible. Cooked foods lose much of their nutrients and minerals and can't pass through our bodies quickly enough for proper elimination. Phyllis A. Balach and Dr. James F. Balach, in *Prescriptions for Cooking*, endorse a vegetarian diet.

> The human digestive system was not designed to digest meat. Compare the time it takes the digestive system to pass vegetarian food with that of meat. Vegetarian food will pass out

of the system in one and a half days, whereas meat will pass out of the body in about five days.

Raw meat is in a state of continual decay. It will contaminate everything it comes into contact with, including the cook's hands. The poisonous bacteria found in raw meat are frequently not even destroyed when the meat is undercooked, barbecued, or roasted. These are source of infection.[4]

Pork is not food for our nourishment. I remember my grandmother saying that pork was to be cooked well done. The Food and Drug Administration told this to the public in an effort to destroy the worms known to be alive in swine meat.

You can cook pork until it's over-cooked, and these worms (which can't be seen with the natural eye) will continue to live in your body, feeding off your cells and waste. I strongly recommend that you become informed about what you have been consuming.

Studies have proven that the African diet of American food is not conducive to good health. Our genetic make-up is still tied to Africa, and we must go back to our natural cycle of life and abandon this cycle of death.

A Toxic Body

We have a recent testimony of one of our ministers who received a colonic irrigation treatment and lost ten pounds overnight. Colonics remove the waste from the colon that's been there for many years. An impacted colon can weight 85 pounds by itself!

Most diseases can be traced to a dirty or toxic body. The longer this poison remains in you, the greater your chances of contracting disease. These toxic poisons will attack the organs of your body and the doctors will either put you on a machine, medicate you, or cut it out.

Another one of our sisters recently discovered that her constant migraine headaches were caused by a toxic body. The cure will be simple. She needs to start putting live foods in the body and clean out the toxins that are poisoning her system.

White, refined sugar is another silent killer along with table salt. We have to stop being gullible and eating whatever is handed to us.

I believe we must go to God in prayer. If we are truly seeking the Word of God, we will find the answer. Those who persistently ask, seek, and knock will be satisfied in their quest (Matthew 7:7,8).

Some things are spiritual and must be handled in the spirit realm. Other things can be handled naturally by simply obeying the laws of nature. Author Toni Toney sums it up with this principle:

> The law of nature is very simple: We are born in this earth to eat food that is grown on this earth. The more complex we make nutrition, the more complex our disease becomes.[5]

Consider one more thing before we go on. Do you know who benefits from your health coverage? When you get ill your health coverage ensures that those treating you are paid. After the money is gone, you are sent home to die with your family. The smart thing to do is to keep your coverage. Doctors have a prominent place in the medical profession, but we must take greater personal responsibility for our own health. If you don't take care of yourself and your family, who will?

Autointoxication means self-poisoning. Stop poisoning your mind and body with seeds of death. Begin educating yourself with nutritional knowledge. Eat foods with life-giving nutrients.

Corrupted by Sin

Much has been said about who we should be in the eyes of God. We were all created in the image and likeness of God. His original purpose for mankind can be summed up in this verse:

> For whom he did foreknow, he also did predestinate to be conformed to the image of his Son, that he might be the firstborn among many brethren (Romans 8:29).

God knew us before we were born (Jeremiah 1:5). Because we came out of God, we were always in Him. Pregnant with the entire human family, God gave birth to one man and put seed in him that would produce successive generations. When man became corrupt through sin, out of a willful act of disobedience, this seed was contaminated with rebellion against the Creator and His intended purpose for us. So great a distance separated God and His masterpiece, man, that it seemed as though the relationship was over forever.

God sought for someone who could bring salvation to His people and restore the communion and fellowship they once enjoyed with Him. But "he saw that there was no man, and wondered that there was no intercessor" (Isaiah 59:16). No one on this earth was found who could destroy the breach between God and His creation.

The only one who could qualify to redeem us would have to be someone in our likeness who hadn't taken on the corruption of the seed that was originally sown (1 Peter 1:23-25).

God is spirit, and the man He created is spirit as well.

The word *human* has a couple of meanings. The first part of this word, *hu,* is a Latin root akin to *humus,* meaning earth, ground, or soil. The word *hue* means dark colored; also original general appearance. Looking closely at the word human we can see first the soil. Since man is spirit like God, a human would be man (spirit) in soil (body).

We can also infer the color of the human is dark like the soil. This lines up with the scientific discovery that all colors can be produced by black and no colors can be produced by white. We may have learned this in art class, but God knew this when He created man in Africa.

The spirit, which is man, was corrupted through disobedience in the African/Edenic man. Every seed that came from him was also corrupted in the eyes of God and in need of redemption.

The prefix *re* means back or again and *deem* means to buy. We already belonged to God, but we were sold into sin and corruption and needed to be purchased again or redeemed.

Because the first seed was corrupted, we needed an incorruptible seed to destroy the effects of the first seed and reestablish a new generation of righteous seeds. Remember that God made seeds to reproduce after their own kind. What does that mean? The seed of the first man Adam, if not abolished, would continue to produce corruption forever. That's why God had to intervene in our salvation. No one on earth could do the job.

If you're having trouble understanding this, stay with me for just a few minutes. These truths are vital to your soul being redeemed to God. Our salvation is intertwined with God's miraculous intervention. A virgin birth. A sinless life. A man raised from the dead. Don't stumble over these essential truths.

Redeemed by God

If God is God, can He put a seed in a woman that He made? Can He put Himself in the seed that He made? Can God walk in the same kind of body that He created and still remain who He is? Because the man sinned, it was going to take another man to undo what the first had done.

> And without controversy great is the mystery of godliness: God was manifest in the flesh, justified in the Spirit, seen of angels, preached unto the Gentiles, believed on in the world, received up into glory (1 Timothy 3:16).

There is no controversy or opposing argument. This is the ultimate of all truth! God manifested Himself in the likeness of sinful flesh to redeem His creation back to Himself (Romans 8:3).

Why did blood have to be shed? Blood being shed represents life being taken, for "the life of the flesh is in the blood" (Leviticus 17:11). Under the old covenant the law required a life for a life (Deuteronomy 19:21). Without the shedding of blood, there is no remission or pardon for sin (Hebrews 9:22).

The blood and life of sacrificial animals was innocently shed for the sin of man to cover us and make a way for us to commune with God. The wages of sin is death (Romans 6:23). Death, the taking of life, was the price for the sin that the first man committed. These sacrifices were only substitutes. Because man sinned, man had to pay the wages of that sin, which was death.

The sacrifice had to be incorruptible, meaning the seed could not come from planet earth.

God took back from Satan what was rightfully His. No man could do it because all have sinned and come short of the glory of God. God used His Own arm to bring salvation to the human family (Isaiah 59:16).

A Return to Eden

Man is spirit, therefore his spirit is in need of regeneration.

The word regenerate is an interesting word. *Re* means back or again and *generate* means to produce (offspring); beget; procreate. *Genus*, which is part of the original word generate, means to birth, origin, race, species, kind.

To be regenerate means to be birthed like the original race, species, or kind again.

This is the original man or spirit being birthed just like he was originally in paradise. This happens as we connect with God who has manifested Himself as Jesus Christ. When we receive what God has done through Christ, we are regenerated. Our spirit is reconciled to God's Spirit. The original man can take his proper place in the earth that was created for him to rule. We can't be what we were intended to be without being connected to the source of life.

Romans 8:29 says that God "did predestinate [us] to be conformed to the image of his Son, that He might be the first-born among many brethren."

Our destiny was set before (predestinated) to be conformed (fashioned, formed) to the image of God, manifested in flesh. Jesus Christ became the firstborn of the original race that God predestined.

What the first man corrupted, Christ redeemed. He brought death to the corruption and became the firstborn of an incorruptible race.

And so it is written, The first man Adam was made a living soul; the last Adam was made a quickening spirit; Howbeit that was not first which is spiritual, but that which is natural; and afterward that which is spiritual. The first man is of the earth, earthy: the second man is the Lord from heaven (1 Cor. 15:45-47).

This passage speaks about a first man who is of the earth and a second man who is the Lord from heaven. The second man is not from this earth. It would have been unlawful for God to come to earth in any form other than man. Why? Because He said the earth was for the dominion of man. Only man has the legal right to be on this earth, and God will not go against His word. That's why He came in the likeness of sinful flesh – but without sin – and redeemed mankind back to Himself.

A first and second man implies a third man. The third man is the redeemed race that the second man came to redeem.

Will you consider our Savior Jesus Christ and His wonderful redemption? I pray you'll receive Him as Savior and Lord today. Write me and let me know what you have decided to do.

Only those who have been redeemed can produce the fruit of righteousness. When God Himself lives inside you, you'll be able to love your enemies. Instead of lashing out in hate and anger at your oppressors, you can live a Spirit-controlled life. When you respond to racism with goodness and patience, it testifies of the life-changing power of Jesus Christ.

What are you producing?

Epilogue

Until oppressors cease from their oppression of non-white people and stop talking about equality and start producing true equal opportunities, the need to confront such issues will remain among us.

Black people all over the world have never wanted anything other than to be what God purposed for them to be – people who would be treated with respect and sensitivity for our plight under European domination.

I praise God for the many true Christian white brethren who have honestly and sincerely allowed the Holy Spirit to change their hearts, enabling them to embrace their black brethren all over this country and abroad.

Racism and prejudice will not be eradicated until men submit to the truth and allow it to soften their hearts, removing the deceit.

We, the descendants of Africans, can protest, work hard, and rally for proper treatment in the world. These things won't last, however, until we are liberated from the spirit of depending on someone else to supply us with what is vital to our survival.

We can't change the heart of our oppressors, but we can certainly change ourselves! As Dr. Myles Munroe says, "You can't legislate laws to change a man's heart."

Focusing on what God can do in the hearts and lives of men, the prophet Ezekiel gives us hope:

I will sprinkle clean water on you, and you will be clean; I will cleanse you from all your impurities and from all your idols. I will give you a new heart and put a new spirit in you; I will remove from you your heart of stone and give you a heart of flesh. And I will put my Spirit in you and move you to follow my decrees and be careful to keep my laws (Ezekiel 36:25-27, NIV).

Only God, through the power of His Holy Spirit, can cause a man to receive in love someone he once hated and despised. Those at enmity because of race can be bonded together by our Creator.

We can't keep running from the truth. It is important to recognize that African people did not conceal and rewrite history. African people were not responsible for the attempted destruction of the sphinx in Egypt to cover up the great accomplishments of our race. African people were not the initiators of race class distinctions. The truth is resurfacing. Let's stop making excuses and just do what is right to correct the wrong.

Through much love and prayer, all of us must become messengers of the truth. Truth will give us a new heart with the law of love inscribed upon it. Truth will enable us to one day put down subjects such as racism and pick up love and unity, forever embracing them.

Love your neighbor as you love yourself.

Endnotes

Introduction

1. Benjamin B. Wolman, *Dictionary of Behavioral Science* (Van Nostrand Reinhold Company), p. 397.
2. F. Earle Fox, *Biblical Inner Healing* (Ambridge, PA: Emmanus Ministries, 1993), p. 48.
3. *Webster's New World Dictionary* (Third College Edition, 1988).
4. Fox, p. 79.

Chapter 1

1. Stan DeKoven, Ph.D., *I Want to be Like You Dad* (Ramona, CA: Vision Publishing, 1994), pp. 34.
2. Fox, p. 55.
3. Thomas Verny, M.D., *The Secret Life of the Unborn Child* (New York: Dell Publishing, 1981), pp. 61.
4. Ibid., p. 47.
5. Ibid., pp. 67,68.
6. Drs. George and Yvonne Abatso, *How to Equip the African American Family* (Chicago: Urban Ministries, Inc., 1991), p. 13.

Chapter 2

1. James Strong, *Strong's Exhaustive Concordance of the Bible* (Iowa Falls, IA: Riverside Book and Bible House), Reference number 3053.
2. Leanne Payne, *Restoring the Christian Soul Through Healing Prayer* (Wheaton, IL: Crossway Books, 1991), p. 27.
3. Ibid., pp. 31,32.
4. John and Paula Sanford, *Restoring the Christian Family* (Tulsa, OK: Victory House, Inc., 1979), p. 98.

5. Payne, *Restoring the Christian Soul*, p. 41.
6. Abatso, pp. 13,28,29,31.
7. Amos N. Wilson, *The Developmental Psychology of the Black Child* (New York: African Research Publications, 1978), p. 9.
8. Torrance Mathis, *The Politics of Self, The Living Constitution* (Los Angeles: MST Publishing, 1992), p. 31.
9. Na'im Akbar, Ph.D., *Chains & Images of Psychological Slavery* (Jersey City, NY: New Mind Productions, 1984), p. 22.
10. Amos N. Wilson, *Black-on-Black Violence* (Brooklyn, NY: Afrikan World Info Systems, 1990), p. 63.
11. *Webster's New World Dictionary*, Third College Edition, 1988.
12. Wilson, *Black-on-Black Violence*, p. 56.
13. Ibid.
14. Dr. Frances Cress Welsing, *The Isis Papers* (Chicago: Third World Press, 1991), pp. 166,168.
15. Akbar, *Chains & Images*, p. 52.
16. Dr. Edwin J. Derensbourg, *The Roots of Deliverance* (Lancaster, CA: Published by author, 1994), pp. 96,97.

Chapter 3

1. Wilson, *The Developmental Psychology*, p. 9.
2. *Webster's New World Dictionary*, Third College Edition, 1988.
3. Dr. Carter G. Woodson, *The Miseducation of the Negro* (Nashville, TN: Winston-Derek Publishers, Inc., 1990), p. 20.
4. Ibid., p. 27.
5. Carlisle John Peterson, *The Destiny of the Black Race* (Toronto, Canada: Lifeline Communications, 1991), pp. 18,19.
6. Fox, p. 73.

7. Woodson, *The Miseducation of the Negro*, p. 131.
8. Dr. Larry Crabb, *Effective Biblical Counseling* (Grand Rapids, MI: Zondervan Publishing Company), p. 156.
9. Wilson, *The Developmental Psychology*, p. 78.
10. Wilson, *Black on Black Violence*, p. 81.
11. Dr. Mensa Otabil, *Beyond the Rivers of Ethiopia* (Bakersfield, CA: Pneuma Life Publishing, 1993), p. 12,13.
12. Peterson, p. 119.

Chapter 4

1. Derensbourg, p. 93.
2. Fox, p. 76.
3. Ibid.
4. Dr. Jawanza Kunjufu, *Developing Positive Self-Images & Discipline in Black Children* (Chicago: African American Images, 1994), p. 27.
5. Crabb, p. 61.
6. Wilson, *The Developmental Psychology*, p. 131.
7. Leanne Payne, *Crisis in Masculinity* (Wheaton, IL: Crossway Books, 1978), p. 89.
8. Wilson, *Black-on-Black*, p. 96.
9. Payne, p. 88.

Chapter 5

1. John and Paula Sanford, *The Transformation of the Inner Man* (Tulsa, OK: Victory House, 1982), pp. 302,303.
2. Dr. Jawanza Kunjufu, *Countering the Conspiracy to Destroy Black Boys, Volume II* (Chicago: African American Images, 1986), p. 3.
3. Robert Hicks, *The Masculine Journey* (Navpress Books), p. 99.

Chapter 6

1. Stan DeKoven, Ph.D., *On Belay* (Ramona, CA: Vision Publishing, 1994), p. 78.
2. Welsing, p. 166,168.
3. Chief Musamaali-Nangoli, *No More Lies About Africa*, Third Reprint (East Orange, NJ: African Heritage Publishers, 1987), p. 45.

Chapter 7

1. Barry Chant, *The Church* (Published by the author, 1988), p. 1.
2. Dr. Jawanza Kunjufu, *Why Black Men Don't Go To Church* (Chicago: African American Images, 1994), pp. 66,67.
3. Na'im Akbar, *Visions for Black Men* (Tallahassee, FL: New Mind Productions & Associates, 1991), p. 15.

Chapter 8

1. Fox, p. 45.
2. Wilson, *The Developmental Psychology*, p. 85.
3. Myles Munroe, *In Pursuit of Purpose* (Shippensburg, PA: Destiny Image, 1992), pp. 77-79.
4. DeKoven, *I Want to Be Like You Dad*, p. 92,93.

Chapter 9

1. DeKoven, *I Want to Be Like You Dad*, p. 39.
2. Wilson, *The Developmental Psychology*, p. 7.
3. Ibid., p. 33.
4. Phyllis A. Balach, C.N. and James F. Balach, M.D., *Prescription for Cooking* (Greenfield, IN: PAB Books Publishing, Inc., 1987), p. 146.
5. Toni Toney, *Re-Alk-Alive Diet for the New Millennium* (Compiled by Toni Toney).

Pneuma Life Publishing

The African Cultural Heritage Topical Bible

The African Cultural Heritage Topical Bible is a quick and convenient reference Bible. It has been designed for use in personal devotions as well as group Bible studies. It's the newest and most complete reference Bible designed to reveal the Black presence in the Bible and highlight the contributions and exploits of Blacks from the past to present. It's a great tool for students, clergy, teachers — practically anyone seeking to learn more about the Black presence in Scripture, but didn't know where to start. *The African Cultural Heritage Topical Bible* contains:

• Over **395** easy to find **topics**
• **3,840 verses** that are systematically organized
• A comprehensive listing of Black Inventions
• Over **150 pages** of Christian Afrocentric articles on Blacks in the Bible, Contributions of Africa, African Foundations of Christianity, Culture, Identity, Leadership, and Racial Reconciliation written by Myles Munroe, Wayne Perryman, Dr. Leonard Lovett, Dr. Trevor L. Grizzle, James Giles, and Mensa Otabil.
Available in the **New International Version** and the **King James Version**.

The Minister's Topical Bible

by Derwin Stewart

The Minister's Topical Bible covers every aspect of the ministry providing quick and easy access to Scriptures in a variety of ministry related topics. This handy reference tool can be effectively used in leadership training, counseling, teaching, sermon preparation, and personal study.

The Believer's Topical Bible

by Derwin Stewart

The Believer's Topical Bible covers every aspect of a Christian's relationship with God and man, providing biblical answers and solutions for many challenges. It is a quick, convenient, and thorough reference Bible that has been designed for use in personal devotions and group Bible studies. With over 3,800 verses systematically organized under 240 topics, it is the largest devotional-topical Bible available in the **New International Version** and the **King James Version.**

The 1993 Trial on the Curse of Ham

by Wayne Perryman

Is the Black race cursed? This trial, attended by over 450 people, was the first time in over 3,000 years Ham had an opportunity to tell his side of the story and explain exactly what took place in the tent of his father, Noah. The evidence submitted by the defense on behalf of Ham and his descendants was so powerful that it shocked the audience and stunned the jury. Evidence presented by the defense was supported by over 442 biblical references.

Beyond the Rivers of Ethiopia

by Mensa Otabil

Beyond the Rivers of Ethiopia is a powerful and revealing look into God's purpose for the Black race. It gives scholastic yet simple answers to questions you have always had about the Black presence in the Bible. At the heart of this book is a challenge and call to the offspring of the Children of Africa, both on continent and throughout the world, to come to grips with their true identity as they go *Beyond the Rivers of Ethiopia.*

Why? Because You Are Anointed
by T.D. Jakes
Like the eternal nature of ocean tides, the question, why?, always comes back. There seem to be as many reasons to ask why as there are grains of sand on the beach. And yet, like the tide, God brings the answers and washes our questions away. *Workbook also available*

Help Me! I've Fallen
by T.D. Jakes
"Help! I've fallen, and I can't get up." This cry, made popular by a familiar television commercial, points out the problem faced by many Christians today. Have you ever stumbled and fallen with no hope of getting up? Have you been wounded and hurt by others? Are you so far down you think you'll never stand again? Don't despair. All Christians fall from time to time. Life knocks us off balance, making it hard – if not impossible – to get back on our feet. The cause of the fall is not as important as what we do while we're down. T.D. Jakes explains how – and Whom – to ask for help. In a struggle to regain your balance, this book is going to be your manual to recovery! Don't panic. This is just a test!

Becoming A Leader
by Myles Munroe
Many consider leadership to be no more than staying ahead of the pack, but that is a far cry from what leadership is. Leadership is deploying others to become as good as or better than you are. Within each of us lies the potential to be an effective leader. *Becoming A Leader* uncovers the secrets of dynamic leadership that will show you how to be a leader in your family, school, community, church and job. No matter where you are or what you do in life this book can help you to inevitably become a leader. Remember: it is never too late to become a leader. As in every tree there is a forest, so in every follower there is a leader. *Workbook also available*

Available at your local bookstore

Visit our web page at http://www.pneumalife.com